PRAISE FOR THE BLUE CABIN

'Michael Faulkner has composed a prose hymn to
Strangford Lough – with a dash of *The Good Life* thrown in.
He creates a wonderful sense of place, a keenly and sensitively
observed picture of the lough in all its moods, of the wildlife
and the characters who live round the shore.
As a bonus, there is an affectionate picture of the home life
of a prominent statesman and a tightly knit family.
This book is a little gem.'

Maurice Hayes, author of *Sweet Killough, Let Go Your Anchor*

'A tale of life restored on a small island; frank, funny and innocent.'

Olivia O'Leary, broadcaster

'To put an improbable Ulster romantic and his artist-wife
on a small island in an Irish lough was certain to
produce an enthralling book.'

John Cole, former BBC political editor

'An enchanting, funny, touching book.'

Belfast Telegraph

'Charmingly written … a moving account.'

Down Recorder

'Lovers of this unique part of Northern Ireland
will be enthralled and delighted by this book.'

Mourne Observer

'Beautifully written.'

BBC Radio Ulster

To Patricia Ross —

Best wishes,

THE BLUE CABIN

Living by the tides on Islandmore

MICHAEL
FAULKNER

BLACKSTAFF
PRESS
———
BELFAST

First published in September 2006 by
Blackstaff Press
4c Heron Wharf, Sydenham Business Park
Belfast, BT3 9LE
with the assistance of
The Arts Council of Northern Ireland

Reprinted 2006, 2007, 2009, 2010

Typeset by CJWT Solutions, St Helens, Merseyside

Printed in Great Britain by the MPG Books Group

A CIP catalogue record for this book is available from the
British Library

ISBN 978-0-85640-793-2

www.blackstaffpress.com
www.thebluecabin.com

To my mother,
who pushed gently from behind;
and my father, from above.

Prologue

On a Thursday morning we had spelling, and if you didn't get seventeen out of twenty, you were caned. Sometimes I scraped it but more often than not I found myself, along with Black II, Fumphy Friars and a serial misspeller named Denny Gibson, whose only mistake, it's frightening to speculate, was to be born dyslexic, bending over in front of the class for three of the best. I would cry a little, and afterwards I would run outside and round the back of the hedge to the woodworking shed for some comfort and solace from Willie Edgar, the school carpenter.

Willie was always making something and I always said, 'What are you making?' and he always said: 'A seebackroscope.'

'What does it do?'

'It's so you can see backwards.'

'Why?'

'Because we don't always know where we're going, so it's nice to know where we've been.'

'Can you make one for me?'

He would look down at me with a serious face, his spectacles off kilter and misted with fine sawdust, and shake his head.

'I could,' he would say. 'But it's a lot better to have two.'

I knew the answer to my next question very well but I loved to hear it anyway.

'Why?'

'Because if you take two seebackroscopes and mount them back to back, you can look through one and into the other, and see the future.

It's a double seebackroscope. Gives you something to look forward to.'

I was old enough to suspect that he wasn't being serious and young enough to hope that he was. Either way, from the point of view of impressing my friends, a seebackroscope sounded like a really good thing to have. I made Willie promise one day to build me a pair of them, and every time I ran into him after that I would ask if they were ready.

'I'm working on it,' he always said. 'They're on the bench.'

A couple of years went by without any sign of my seebackroscopes, and then something awful happened. When the time came to leave Mourne Grange, I went without saying goodbye to Willie Edgar. Afterwards I felt a terrible guilt, and to make matters worse, I convinced myself that the seebackroscopes were to have been his leaving present to me; that if I had just popped round to the shed, he would have been waiting for me, standing with his back to the workbench, holding something the size of a shoebox, wrapped in newspapers.

I'll never know. Soon after I left, Mourne Grange closed for good. I went on to another boarding school much further from home, and sadly Willie passed away some years ago – taking, I expect, the secret of the double seebackroscope with him.

Thirty-eight years on, I still think of him now and then, especially when I'm struggling to put things in perspective. I think I understand better now what he meant, and in lieu of the real thing I have contrived a pair of virtual seebackroscopes, which I use, with mixed results, to temper a dangerous tendency to dwell in the past. Such optimism as I possess is not innate, as my father's was, but acquired, albeit at the tender age of ten; and good old Willie Edgar, as a consequence, has earned himself a permanent place next to my father in my personal gallery of heroes.

One

During a long and fretful night, when every small sound seemed to echo through the cheerless and empty rooms around us, we lay close and slept hardly at all. In the morning we settled the dogs in the car, found some room for the very last things out of the house in a cardboard box with 'Island' scrawled on the side, heaved the box into the van and left Quilchena for the last time.

Tried to leave anyway. We were all set, but to my shame it hadn't occurred to me that we would not actually be able to go together. I should have made sure the car was in Edinburgh, even along the road; perhaps then it would have been less painful. Perhaps the two of us could have jumped into the van and headed down the lane without looking back. As it was, neither of us seemed ready to make the first move and we shuffled awkwardly and silently about, wandering in and out of the courtyard, checking the sheds and the garden, double-checking the house. Delaying. We hardly looked at one another, tried not to look at anything probably, and we said little. Bewildered and panicked that the moment had finally come, we were past words, but we each knew that with every step we drew on the other's reserves of strength, and of course we should have been together when we left.

Eventually, out of excuses, I headed, as I thought, purposefully towards the van. Looking back at Lynn I tried to say something, no doubt less than helpful, like 'Let's go then', but I have a tendency to mumble which is much worse in stressful situations. 'Lengo thany hon eh,' I said, and jerked my head over my shoulder, thumbing inanely in the direction of the road. When she opened the car door to get in,

I climbed up into the van to drive ahead of her out of the courtyard, but there was no sign of her in the rear-view mirror, so I stopped and walked back.

She was sitting with the engine running, clutching the steering wheel with one white-knuckled hand, a sodden handkerchief in the other. Tears flowed freely from the point of her chin. Her fist – her whole forearm – glistened. She was unable to bring herself to drive away.

Looking down at her, I felt the same cocktail of emotions – tenderness, guilt, fear – that had given me sleepless nights for months. Guilt especially. It was not, after all, her fault that it had come to this: her business had not failed. If anything, her career had been gaining momentum. Demand from the galleries for her work, hard to satisfy at the best of times, had not let up just because we were in difficulties, and she had felt, I think, that it was more important than ever to maintain some kind of continuity, for sanity as much as for cash flow. So against the odds she had worked on until just a few weeks before the move, alternately painting and filling packing cases in her studio. Somehow she managed to keep creating even as the wall of boxes grew around her, until eventually she disappeared behind it. Embattled but steadfast, her work became more than ever an escape and she continued to fulfil commitments, turning down nothing and miraculously, it seemed to me, finding from somewhere within herself the inspiration to keep producing work of real quality.

And for many months she had watched helplessly while I exhausted myself in a series of futile fire-fighting exercises to try to save the business, the house, the reassuring pattern of our lives; stitching together one refinancing package after another, living on borrowed time and money, dreaming of better days – stumbling into insolvency. For almost two years she had hung over the precipice to which I had led her and it seemed exquisitely unfair that at this crucial moment she should be asked to cut the rope herself, to freefall into the darkness that seemed to be our future.

In the emotional charge of those last minutes, as she tried to summon the courage to drive away from her beloved Quilchena – the one place where her personal life and artistic life had truly come together, perhaps the most meaningful expression of her creative energies, certainly the answer to an instinctive and uncompromising nest-building yen that had been a driving force since childhood –

everything seemed out of proportion. The simple act of pressing on the accelerator had become the ultimate act of will. An instant was an age.

She looked up and started to say, 'I don't want …'; and in those words, I believe, lay the worst pain of all. *I don't want to leave my Dad.* On the other side of the courtyard archway was the one remaining place that held any meaningful connection with her father, where the two of them had walked the same ground and breathed the same air. The catalyst had been a shared passion for growing things and a boundless appetite, on Lynn's part, to learn; and the vegetable garden they created together had become their private meeting place, filled for eight precious years with their laughter and their love. After her father had gone, that's where she would go to find him, and now that she was leaving Quilchena she was saying goodbye all over again. It felt, to her, like a double bereavement.

I had a moment of inspiration. Our nearest neighbour, and in recent weeks our most dependable visitor at Quilchena, had been a formidable five-year-old called Sam Hawkins. Having been uprooted from friends, and as far as he was concerned all things safe and familiar, by his parents'

move from Edinburgh that spring, Sam found himself standing at Big Crossroads of Life and turned his small steps with characteristic purpose towards Quilchena; specifically towards Lynn. They became firm friends, and in terms of moral support, to some extent mutually dependent. Aware, because she had been at pains to explain it to him, that his new best friend would soon be leaving for a distant and mysterious Island, Sam was persuaded by a plan cooked up between Lynn and his parents that it would actually be a Good Thing: as soon as we knew our completion date, plane tickets were booked for his first trip to come and stay, and Lynn looked out a photograph of the cabin where we intended to live, over which she and Sam made plans for  all those swimming, boating and exploring adventures to come.

Meantime, and to Lynn's eternal gratitude, Sam fell into an unchanging routine. Every morning he would pull his wellingtons over his pyjamas, sometimes leaving the house before his father, who commuted to Edinburgh, and set off on a commute of his own, skirting round the sheep field, climbing the stock fence with its top strand of barbed wire, running through the shrub bed, across the back yard, round the side of the steading and up to the kitchen door, where he would skid to a halt and knock politely before entering to take up his position, breathless and expectant, at the table next to the Aga. Normally I was the first one down and would pour myself another cup of coffee and fetch Sam's breakfast – apple juice and pitta bread. The two of us would chat about this and that until Lynn appeared, and by the time I left for work they would be hard at it, lugging boxes to the studio or scrap timber to the eternal bonfire at the back of the house – a tireless and close-knit team of two.

I don't think it's an exaggeration to say that Sam's visits were crucial in helping Lynn through a difficult time. While he was there, she remained positive; whether for or because of him, even she doesn't know. Probably both. In any case, Sam came into my mind as we agonised in the courtyard, and I suggested we call in to see him, tell him cheerio; we could always pop back to the house in ten minutes if we had forgotten something.

Lynn nodded, took a deep breath. A familiar and reassuring look of determination came over her face, and soon our little convoy was bouncing off down the lane.

Of course, we never did go back.

Two

Looking at it later, and even at the time in less self-absorbed moments, we felt foolish that while others had graver issues to deal with – illness, divorce, bereavement – we should have been so devastated by the loss of what one friend called 'only bricks and mortar'. And I have to say it is hard to explain. Back in 1990 business was good. We had both had enough of city life and were engaged to be married. We went looking for a cottage, with modest enough expectations: two bedrooms, a garden, preferably something close to water. A place where black cabs were unlikely to sit below the bedroom window at three in the morning with their engines running, but no more than forty-five minutes from Edinburgh.

I telephoned my lawyer to ask him to keep an eye open. As it happened, he had taken instructions from a client to divide up his Kinross-shire farm and sell it in lots. Most of the land had already gone privately to neighbouring farms but the house itself, with a few acres, had not yet been marketed. Would I be interested in having a look before it was advertised? It sounded on the big side but I said, 'Absolutely', and Lynn and I drove out the same day.

We were given a draft set of particulars: a single A4 sheet with no photograph and only the sketchiest description. 'Secluded farmhouse with steading courtyard … in need of some modernisation. Forty minutes from Edinburgh, in the first unspoilt valley north of the Forth estuary. Approx. 18 acres.' There was a photocopied Ordnance Survey map on the back, with directions. We should go four miles off the motorway and look for a lane to the left, lined with oak trees.

It was a foul February afternoon. The sky was dark and full, and snow at the road edges was turning to slush in heavy rain. As we left the motorway we had occasional glimpses of Nivingston Crags, a sheer wall of sandstone half a mile to our left, rising five hundred feet from the valley floor and marking the northern limit of Cleish Hills. Further out to north and west, the faint outlines of the Ochil and Lomond Hills hinted at a wildness neither of us had anticipated. Lynn looked over at me. She nodded and smiled, and I knew what she meant. It was like Alice and the looking glass: half a mile back we had shared six lanes of grey and featureless asphalt with the rest of humanity and we seemed now to have passed seamlessly into another world.

The feeling persisted when we found the lane and turned in. Clearly it hadn't seen use for some hours because the snow lay undisturbed, a carpet of white running straight ahead between the tall, rusted-copper lines of two beech hedges. Leafless trees rose at intervals on either side and at the far end we could see the stone-built corner of the house, or perhaps the steading.

And really that was it. We felt as though we were arriving home.

What we had seen from the road turned out to be one arm of a U-shaped steading, which together with the house itself formed the four sides of a courtyard big enough to turn a car in. There was room for a studio, workshop, garage, and all the storage we would ever need in the outbuildings.

The house was quite small, with rubble walls of ochre sandstone and grey whin. Originally a two-room cottage, an extra half-storey had been squeezed into the roof space and Victorian extensions had been added to each end at opposing right angles, giving the place a quirky, rather haphazard feel inside, with unexpected returns and corridors, as though it had evolved organically at the whim of seven or eight generations of occupants. Outside, an overgrown paddock led down past a bothy cottage to a burn, which formed the south boundary, and on all sides there were open views across meadow and farmland to the hills. It was charming and, best of all, the nearest house was a quarter of a mile away.

For us it was a blank canvas that we gave the best part of five years to filling. We started with the house and by the end almost nothing of the internal layout remained, several bedrooms and all the corridors falling to our somewhat obsessive quest for open spaces, for a blending of living area and landscape as seamless as the Scottish winter would allow. In more than a passing nod to Santa Fe style, which we first saw in a friend's house in Santa Monica in 1989, this meant not only access and sightlines to the outside at all available points, but a literal echoing of the tones and textures of the countryside on the surfaces within.

This was Lynn's department. When we first wandered round sketching out ideas for the house, I know we were thinking along similar lines – with Lynn's artist's eye and my back-of-an-envelope furniture designs, we have a shared ability to visualise structure and space – but when it comes to seeing the detail of the end result as though it were already in place – the feel, the colour, the atmosphere – Lynn is the master. I did not realise it at the time, but during those first tentative explorations of the possibilities of the house, she was able to visualise ochre- and salmon-washed rough-plastered walls accented with terracotta ceramic tile inserts, pale weathered timber doors and flooring, driftwood lintels and, I wouldn't be surprised, the subtle little Navajo wheat-sheaf motifs she later painted at each end of the massive mantelpiece above the living-room fire.

Proud of what Lynn had achieved, when the remodelling was complete I sent off some slides and the house appeared on the cover of *Period Living* and then in a raft of other interiors magazines. Lynn was mortified, and agreed to each new photo session only for the sake of the PR value to my furniture business.

We called the house Quilchena, after the ranch in British Columbia where I worked during a gap year before law school. The name derives from Native American and French Canadian dialects and means, roughly, 'feather oaks'.

But for me Quilchena is more than a name. It is an aspiration, another life; a dream. My time in Canada as a teenager was perhaps the most fulfilled of my life, and I may have been trying to regain that place in my mind ever since. Quilchena is the frustrated cowboy in me. I have even tried to live the dream in my working life. After brief excursions into law and property, I found an unlikely opportunity to indulge myself in a career in furniture design and retail. In what turned out to be a misjudged and costly, but hugely enjoyable, exercise, we transformed a back alley in a rather genteel residential area of south Edinburgh into a Western township of the mid-1800s, cladding both sides of the 'street' with faithfully detailed false fronts until we had the whole John Ford: saloon, grain store, log house, cantina, livery stables, railroad station and, of course, a sheriff's office.

All this to accommodate a range of furniture of my own design, inspired by the frontier furniture of the American southwest and, as far as I know, the first cohesive collection of its kind in the UK. It was expensive to manufacture and ultimately unprofitable to sell, but six days a week I got to go to my office via Main Street, El Pedro. As word got around I was approached by production companies and photographers, and El Pedro, Morningside, was the unlikely location during the nineties for fashion shoots, music videos and even a couple of television serials.

Sometimes I suppose I worry about myself. It didn't just start with a few months in a bunkhouse in western Canada. When I was seven or eight, we commandeered an old chicken house in the pony paddock of the family home in Seaforde, Northern Ireland. We covered the walls with cowboy and Indian wallpaper and fitted it with stools and a foldout table. Outside there was a bench where I could stretch out and snooze in the noonday sun, a Stetson pulled low over my eyes, fast asleep and fully alert in the manner of all bona fide sons of the saddle. My hand was never far from a holstered silver Colt, which hung on a hook by the door, awaiting the day when I was big enough to have the belt fit snugly around my hips and not slip towards my ankles with every manly stride. A sign nailed above the door said 'DCM Ranch' – for David, Claire and Michael. We used to tie the ponies to a hitching rail outside and there is a photograph somewhere of two trail-weary cowboys and an Indian (Claire, of course – I used to think all Indians were girls because they had long black hair and made high-pitched whooping sounds when they swarmed down off the mesa to terrorise the wagon trains) standing with the DCM in the background, all squinty smiles and sunshine.

Claire, in fact, used to swarm off the hills quite often, bareback Apache-style on Pinky, a little walleyed skewbald who looked the part and could be trusted not to do anything unpredictable. Murmuring endearments to Pinky and annoyingly detached from – possibly even unaware of – the unfolding drama in which she would be expected to play a central role, she would set out on an eccentric and prolonged circumambulation of the chicken house, sometimes disappearing for minutes at a time on the other side of the rhododendrons, no doubt to regroup, while David and I grabbed our guns and took cover inside. A little unnerved, we would wait there in silent anticipation, straining to catch the first tentative war-whoops which we secretly hoped would build to a terrifying crescendo as the enemy came closer. A sliding wooden trap door low down in the back wall, access for bantams in a former life, provided a vantage point from which I could deliver an inexhaustible hail of lead with my six-shooter at relatively close range, and every few minutes, as Claire wandered recklessly into my field of view, I had just moments in which to pick her off one by one, until eventually she alone was left standing. The battle over, if we ragged survivors were in bad humour, she could expect to be summarily scalped, and Pinky claimed as spoils of war. Otherwise, stripped of weapons and dignity, she would be forced at gunpoint to make tea at the foldout table; something from which, it always irked us to discover, she seemed to take a perverse pleasure, laying out cups, saucers and milk jug just so and inviting us to sit quietly on the stools while the tea infused to her satisfaction.

The others, as you would expect, grew tired of cowboy ways, but a little spark had been planted in my subconscious, which life's opportunities have occasionally fanned into flame. The chicken house of my childhood lived again on thirty thousand acres west of the Rockies, in the shape of a bunkhouse shared with two born-again Blackfoot cowboys named Louis 'Denver Colorado' Holmes and Gerry Macaulay. Seduced there by an image of the Old West whose modern equivalent, I was thrilled to discover, is still a way of life, I built a west of my own in that back lane in Edinburgh. And best of all, during ten years of commuting six days a week to work in the city, I got to escape every night along the valley, down the lane, through the courtyard and into our own Quilchena, Quilchena the home ranch, our very own piece of New Mexico and the only slate-roofed, sandstone-built Santa Fe-style farmhouse east of, well, Santa Fe probably.

So all things considered, leaving the house on that October morning was not part of our life plan. In fact, life plans were on hold for the moment. One thing, however, we did know: we would spend the next few months licking our wounds and taking stock in a very different place. If we thought Quilchena was isolated, try an island on an Irish sea lough with only a wooden cabin and no mains electricity. Try oilskins, sea boots and two small boats just to get to the supermarket.

Try a slippery timber jetty on a stormy December night at low tide with a bag of coal in one hand and a gas cylinder in the other.

By a curious set of circumstances we were island-bound, and we may not have felt it at the time, but life does indeed go on. We had expected, I suppose, to live and die at Quilchena but we did have ten contented years there and as everybody knows, big changes bring big rewards. Or as my mother, who knows everything, is fond of saying, Never a door closes …

Three

That there was a convenient island paradise – secluded, uninhabited and rent-free – to which we could escape at all, we owe to the combined efforts, twenty years apart, of my grandfather and my father; and to one of those bizarre chance encounters that seem to happen far from home.

As I remember him, my grandfather, James Faulkner, was quite a character. A born salesman, in 1921 he founded a shirt-making business in Belfast, which he ran very much as a family affair for thirty-five years, in time bringing in my father and my Uncle Dennis on the sales and finance sides respectively. Silver-haired, bespectacled, immaculate – and a lifelong teetotaller – Grandfather might have seemed the classic sober, hard-working Ulster business type, but he had a mischievous sense of humour, an instinctive and opportunistic approach to business and a disarming warmth and openness that belied the restless workings of a shrewd business brain. Apart from a generation-defining moment some years after he had retired, when he woke with a start from a Sunday afternoon fireside snooze, grinned at my very 1969 tie and said, 'Tell me, is *that* psychedelic?', the two things I most vividly associate with him are noise and smell, both of which were overwhelmingly present in the Faulat factory.

My father, Brian Faulkner, handled sales at Faulat for many years, even after becoming Northern Ireland's youngest MP in 1949 at the age of twenty-eight, but to avoid any perceived conflict of interest he resigned from the business after his first ministerial appointment, to Home Affairs, in 1959. He often stopped by the factory, though, until it was sold to Ladybird in 1963, and how exciting it was to be with him when he did. I recall being led by the hand past numberless rows of clattering machines, whose lady operators, as we passed, would turn their heads without pausing and nod and smile and shout 'Mr Brian!' above the din, screwing up their eyes and wrinkling their noses in my direction. I wrinkled my nose too but not as a sign of endearment; the smell was a potent and rather throat-catching combination of starch and steam-heated cotton, linen and wool from the big presses, and though I haven't encountered it since, I know I would recognise it anywhere. Not so very unpleasant really, just memorable.

Grandfather's life was punctuated by crazes. He was easily bored and never could resist the latest thing, something which he must have passed on to me. When Lynn and I wander the supermarket and a new brand of breakfast cereal catches my eye, she looks at me sideways by way of warning but I can't help it – I am genetically predisposed to put the box in the trolley. Grandfather did, though, have two enduring interests and these were taken up with equal enthusiasm by my father and uncle respectively. He kept horses most of his life and so did my father; but his other passion was sailing, and the three of them used to spend summer weekends racing Rivers, Fairys and Glens on Belfast Lough and Strangford Lough.

Over the years Grandfather acquired a succession of ever more impressive yachts, in which he cruised the west coast of Scotland, and it was his sailing that led indirectly to our sojourn on the island. Just before the Second World War he decided on impulse to have a go at farming and bought six islands on Strangford Lough. Two of them, Islandmore and Dunsy, came with habitable houses. The ground had been grazed for generations but had not been turned for many years and after several seasons of profitable but unrelenting effort, fighting the elements to barge machinery over to the islands and oats, barley and potatoes back, while at the same time running the shirt factory in Belfast, the attractions were beginning to pale. The final straw, so to speak, was an especially late and wet harvest season when after numerous abortive attempts at long range to turn, stook and dry the barley, it finally went under cover on Islandmore on Christmas Eve. Scunnered, Grandfather sold everything, including the wooden cabin on Islandmore.

That was 1949. Then in a kindly twist of fate twenty years later, on a caravanning holiday in the far west of Ireland, my father spotted the Northern Ireland registration on a car parked by the side of the road and typically stopped for a chat. It turned out to be Brian Metcalfe, the then owner of the cabin that had passed out of family ownership two decades before. Not only that, it was shortly to go on the market again. My father couldn't believe his ears and the upshot was that he managed to buy it back; the cabin passed to my mother on my father's death and when Lynn and I needed a base from which to review our options for the future, my mother generously made it available to us.

It had been a most fortuitous, Lynn would say *meant*, encounter, and my father knew that he had acquired in the cabin a one-off gem in a largely unspoilt corner of Ireland. What he could not know was how much importance, in the next phase of his political career, the place would assume. For the family as a whole it was, and remains, a reason to come together, but for my father it also provided a periodic, if rather brief, respite from the daily pressures of life in the 'political hot seat' of Europe. In the days before mobile phones an island was an island, and even taking into account the police presence, the bulging briefcase and the great weight of his political responsibilities, every time my father stepped into a small boat to make the crossing to Islandmore he was able, in some sense, to leave politics behind.

Strangford Lough is on Northern Ireland's east coast, with Belfast Lough to the north and the glorious Mourne Mountains to the south. It lies north–south and is almost twenty miles long and three to four wide, enclosed to the east by the curving arm of the Ards peninsula and open to the Irish Sea only at its extreme southern tip, where on a twelve-hour tidal cycle it receives and expels four hundred million tons of water through a steep-sided channel so narrow that the current reaches eight knots, and the ferry that crosses between Strangford village and Portaferry is forced to strike a crab-wise diagonal to make the landing ramp, aiming several hundred yards upstream from where she means to go.

My very earliest memory of the lough is from a family outing to picnic on the sands at Kilclief. As we passed by the Narrows my father pointed out the car window and said, 'They call that Pullandbedamnedtoyou!' and everybody laughed except me. It was an odd and very long name for a place, I could see that, but not especially funny, and if I only vaguely got the point at the time, it was well made some years later when I found myself heading north against the current in a rather underpowered boat, and looked at the shoreline to find that I was moving backwards.

When Norse raiders first entered the lough from the open sea in the ninth century, we can assume they had to wait for an incoming tide, and the words *strong* and *fjord* must have slipped off the tongue when they put their heads together for a name. The earlier, Irish name, though, was Loch Cuan (*cuan* meaning 'harbour' or 'haven'), which much better describes the main body of water to the north. Surrounded by fertile drumlin hills of glacial boulder clay, for which, in geological terms, east Down is quite famous, the overall impression of the lough as it opens out above the Narrows is of a tranquil and hospitable waterway dotted with rocks, pladdies and grassy, boulder-fringed little islands; a yachtsman's paradise and the perfect place to explore. The shoreline is indented by intimate tidal inlets flanked by rounded headlands and, remarkably, stretches to 150 miles as a result. A concentration of larger islands, themselves the topmost tips of submerged drumlins left behind when the ice retreated ten thousand years ago, ranges along the western shore.

The largest inland sea in the British Isles, Strangford is a place of beguiling variety, millpond-flat one moment, the next whipped by wind and tide in opposition into a wilful, white-topped mêlée capable of putting even sizeable boats to the test. Caught out in a small boat in certain parts of the lough, on an ebb tide with a freshening wind from the southwest, the horizon and all points of reference can disappear altogether behind a black wall of sea, and a vexed, lonely and very small feeling can unexpectedly begin to inform your understanding of a life on the ocean wave.

As a footnote to my father's chance encounter with Brian Metcalfe in Connemara, on one of my trips to the mainland some months after coming to live on Islandmore I saw a little gathering of yachting types on the slipway. Their uncharacteristically raised voices and animated gestures told me something was up, and it turned out that a nocturnal visitor had made off with various equipment from the boat park, including some outboards. The conversation had to do with security and, in particular, locking bars for outboard motors, which were a new idea to me. When I enquired, I was offered a padlock and bar by an affable grey-haired character who had a spare in the boot of his car. We didn't know each other and he asked if I kept a yacht amongst the moorings. I pointed to the dinghy tied up to the pontoon, and to the cabin in the distance.

'No yacht, unfortunately,' I said. 'The dinghy is just to get to the island.'

He smiled broadly and offered his hand.

'Brian Metcalfe,' he said. 'Lucky man!'

break fast.

Four

I have often been told, and very much want to believe, that Strangford Lough has an island for every day of the year, because that would be excellent, but they make the same suspiciously Irish claim about a good many places, including Clew Bay in County Mayo, and it may be one of those country saws that have only relative meanings. I tried to make a count using a straightedge and an Admiralty chart and got to just over a hundred; disappointing, but certainly a lot of islands for one lough, even a big one.

One of the largest, at 120 acres, happens to be Islandmore, where the cabin, originally built for prisoners of war on the Isle of Man, was reassembled section by section in 1921 after the brief sea journey from Douglas. Shaped in plan not unlike a fleeing rabbit at full stretch and lying on a more or less north–south axis within a quarter of a mile of the western shore, the island is around halfway up the lough. The nearest access point from the mainland is reached by a tortuous single track road that passes through an undulating drumlin patchwork of little fields, stone walls and ancient thorn hedges before coming to an abrupt end at an old quay on Ringhaddy Sound. One of the most congenial natural anchorages in the lough, the sound is defined by the close proximity of island to mainland and through the centuries has been a safe haven for Viking longboats, emigrant staging vessels, schooners and steamers carrying coal in, and kelp or farm produce out and, these days, an assortment of yachts, motor sailers and a few small fishing boats.

In the late 1970s Ringhaddy Cruising Club installed floating pontoons and surfaced an area for parking cars and overwintering boats, just along the foreshore from the old quay. Getting to the island became – barring a stiff breeze – a breeze. But things were a good deal more basic in the old days: the family used to keep a plywood punt upturned on a grassy shelf above high-water mark, which we would haul thirty or forty yards over rocks and shingle to the water's edge, depending on the state of the tide. After rowing to something more substantial moored amongst the yachts in the deep water of the sound, we would return to the stone quay to load supplies. For a few years we had a 15-foot dual-hull 'unsinkable' dory, ubiquitous in the lough at that time as a safe, speedy and relatively indestructible workhorse (sadly many of the dories have now been superseded by even more speedy and ubiquitous RIBs, inflatable boats with sometimes inflated ideas of themselves – the 4×4s of the water). Later we upgraded to a 21-foot Dell Quay Fisherboat, a fibreglass workboat with a slow-running in-board diesel from the same stable as the dory. And now, twenty-five years on, there's the Norwegian With (pronounced *Wit*): only 14 foot, with a 25 h.p. Mariner outboard, but built to sail, so with a fair amount of boat below the water line, making for safe, steady going even in a reasonable sea.

Bizarrely the old quay, which was probably built in the late 1700s for the benefit of the local farming and fishing communities, is closed to the public now and mossy grass has established itself between the cobbles. A steel security barrier prevents access to the quay itself and carries a warning sign that is hard to miss:

RINGHADDY PIER

THIS PIER IS THE PRIVATE PROPERTY OF THE

ADJOINING HOUSE

ABSOLUTELY NO ADMITTANCE

Absolutely. I still walk on it from time to time, clambering over the barrier with its rather severe injunction in big black letters. Perhaps vehicular access has been deemed unsafe or, at a stretch, an invasion of privacy, in which case I offer one word: bollards.

It wasn't always like this. Through my teenage years the quay was the family's embarkation point for the island, and Bob Dougal, the self-appointed harbour master who lived in said adjoining house –

then a charming little whitewashed cottage with a corrugated iron roof – made welcome anyone (well, if he liked you, he made you welcome; if not, he tolerated you) who cared to use it for the purpose for which, after all, it had been built: the coming and going of boats.

When I do walk on the quay, I find it is full of ghosts, like the derelict shell of a once vibrant childhood home. I don't have to close my eyes to see my mother, looking fine and happy, organising and watching the rest of us, calling Joe and Matt to heel, three or four blank canvases in one hand and the all-seeing Bell & Howell Standard Eight Cine in the other. I see my father in a cream wool polo neck and navy flannels, hustle-hustle and aglow with pleasure at the prospect of having all the family together for a few days. Claire is close by him as always, laughing, gently teasing him. A newspaper once

referred to the 'slight, silver-haired figure of Brian Faulkner', and with minor embellishments befitting the moment, it was ammunition for the rest of us for years. David is already on the water, rowing out to the Fisherboat, a young man wholly in his element. Then and now, he is Kenneth Grahame's Ratty: 'There is nothing – absolutely nothing – half so much worth doing as simply messing about in boats.' He should have it on his gravestone. Finally, standing off to the side, earnest and watchful, I see Sergeant Bill Connolly. Not strictly one of the family but always a part of it; a benign shadow in the background. When I catch his eye, he gives me an avuncular wink and a nod.

As a government minister, my father always travelled with security and the police escort car would precede us onto the quay when we arrived. Two or three plain-clothes men would emerge and check the place over, but while the others peered into the water off the edge of the quay, or lifted the upturned rowing boat to check underneath, Bill never let my father out of his sight while he was in the open; never, in fact, looked relaxed until we were in the boat and on our way.

When we looked back, he would beam, and wave, a vaguely incongruous figure standing on the edge of the quay: grey suit, white shirt, red tie. I know the smile was genuine, and on more than one account: a safe delivery, of course, but there was also the vicarious pleasure to be had from someone else's enjoyment, someone of whom, I feel confident to say, he was deeply fond.

Out of loyalty and friendship and because, I suspect, he didn't like change any more than I do, my father went to some lengths to keep Bill Connolly with him through three ministerial posts and during his premiership, indeed until his death in 1977, and curiously enough I missed Bill and the others after my father was gone. From a child's perspective the police guard, having been on the scene for as long as I could remember, was a welcome part of our lives, not because the men provided protection but because they were fun to have around. Even my father, for whom it must at times have seemed intolerably claustrophobic, accepted the intrusion without complaint as a fact of political life in Northern Ireland.

Only occasionally did he rebel, like a truant schoolboy, and sneak away from the house at Seaforde for a few hours of freedom with the family. In the summer of 1965, the year of *The Sound of Music*, I came home from school to be told we were all off across the border to County Wexford to look at a horse. It would just, announced my father pointedly, be the family.

'Oh,' I said, and nodded conspiratorially. I would have winked but I was nine.

We packed a picnic – we always packed a picnic – and even before we drove out the gates there was a sense of subversive adventure in the air as we approached the policemen on guard duty in the hut at the end of the drive. For Da there will have been a feeling of guilty pleasure, but for me, sitting on the armrest in the middle of the back seat, this was Austria, not Ulster, and our name was not Faulkner but von Trapp. The guard saluted, passed a few friendly words as usual and raised the barrier to let us through. I knew from the silver insignia glinting off the point of his collar that he was SS, although he looked like Willy John McAlonan, who used to take me to the motorcycle road races on off-duty weekends. As we passed I stared anxiously at him through the rear windscreen, tight-lipped and wide-eyed, inwardly imploring him not to betray us, humming a tuneless

'Edelweiss' and half-expecting him to wheel round in alarm when he noticed there was no escort vehicle and run back into the hut blowing on his whistle and reaching for the radio phone to call HQ. But there was no clatter of jackboots, no machine-gun fire to shatter the windscreen or burst the tyres, and reality returned as we drove on, an anonymous family in an anonymous car.

By our first petrol stop, however, in a small town near the border, any ideas of anonymity were already wearing thin. As we pulled in to the pumps my mother grabbed a tweed hat she had rather hopefully packed as a disguise. She stuck it on my father's silver head, pulling it down low, but in a population as politically aware as the Irish, even before the Troubles, that was a fairly pointless exercise and the car pulling out ahead of us hesitated and stopped. The driver seemed to be staring in the rear-view mirror and saying something to his passenger, who looked back over his shoulder. They got out of the car and the driver leaned down, peering in at us. This might have been the moment, had he been with us, for Bill Connolly to quietly suggest we drive on, no offence, but I honestly don't think that would have occurred to my father. He smiled and nodded in acknowledgement, and recognition seemed to dawn on one of these men because he walked over and thrust out his hand.

'I want to shake this man by the hand!' he said. 'Good to see you!'

His friend joined in with a favourite northern greeting: 'What about you, Brian?'

My mother threw her eyes to heaven as my father stepped out of the car.

'How are you?' he said, making use of another very Irish construction, for which he must have given thanks a thousand times. North or south of the border 'How are you?' works equally well for either 'Nice to meet you' or 'Nice to see you again', which means that when you meet someone and you are almost sure you've never met them before, it is, diplomatically speaking, the greeting of choice. It happened to my father all the time, I think because he was so patently approachable. People liked him because, it was plain to see, he liked people. He could pass the time of day with anyone, and often did. These strangers had come forward because my father had invited them, by the simple courtesy of meeting their eye and smiling, and the three of them stood on the garage forecourt and discussed the issues of the day.

Bill would have had a fit. He always seemed to find out about these rare solo excursions later, probably because my father couldn't resist telling him about them. Da was about as good at that kind of subterfuge as he was at hoodwinking his children when he bumped into one of us in the corridor on Christmas Eve with something mysterious tucked under his coat. That's to say, he wasn't good at it at all. He had no guile, and surprisingly enough that was not an impediment in his political life. In the period leading up to the establishment of the power-sharing Executive in 1974, particularly, when all his energies were directed toward cross-community co-operation as a foundation for peaceful progress in Northern Ireland, it was a positive strength. It is hard to see how anyone else, at the height of the Troubles, could have presided over a governing body where unionists and nationalists worked together at Cabinet level within a proper devolutionary framework. He offered transparent straightness and a focus born of passionate conviction, and was offered trust in return. The Executive may have been short-lived, but only because it was ahead of its time, brought down before it had had a chance to succeed by a combination of hard-line unionism and loyalist paramilitary intimidation in Northern Ireland, and political weakness in Westminster, which together turned a half-hearted localised strike against the new constitution into a wholehearted general one. In 1998 the Good Friday Agreement revisited, to an uncanny extent, the substance of the earlier agreement of which my father had been one of the chief architects.

On the afternoon of 30 May 1974, when events overtook the power-sharing Executive and Direct Rule from Westminster was reimposed by Harold Wilson's Labour government in an atmosphere of vacillation, panic and ultimately capitulation in London, my father looked out over east Belfast from his office in Stormont Castle and spoke to my mother in uncharacteristically despairing terms which reflected, above all, the emotional investment he had made. Hardly one to look back, it was one of the few moments in twenty years of politics that he did. He spoke not so much for himself as for his beloved Ulster: 'The tragedy,' he said, 'is that there will not be another opportunity for twenty years'; and the ensuing quarter century of false starts and missed opportunities proved him tragically right.

the diver

Five

From the day I signed an undertaking with my bank that went on
at length about retention of secured lender's powers, debtors'
obligations, restrictive time limits and the like but could just as easily
have said 'OK, OK. I'll sell the house!' we had to give some thought to
the problem of where to live – cheaply – for the winter and thereafter.

Ireland wasn't necessarily the obvious choice. Most of our friends
and all of Lynn's art contacts, including a number of painters who
were her contemporaries at art college and whose careers had
progressed in parallel with her own, lived in Scotland. The house
contents were in storage in Cowdenbeath in Fife. In a corner of the
same warehouse I had built a small workshop where I hoped to carry
on the only part of the furniture business that had survived, after a
fashion – Santa Fe beds by mail order – and because it was a tiny
concern with no employees, I would need to make regular visits. The
practicality of even a weekly commute, bearing in mind our depleted
resources and the Irish Sea, seemed doubtful.

On the other hand, my family were in Northern Ireland. After so
many years in Scotland it would be good to see more of them. For a
while at least we would be able to live rent-free. And although Lynn
was brought up in a Fife fishing village, during her professional life she
had not had the opportunity to be near the sea and such a complete
change might benefit her work. The clincher, though, was this: it
seemed hardly likely we would ever again have the opportunity to live
through four seasons on an otherwise uninhabited island, in a cabin
used, by and large, as a family bolt hole for a few days at a time

between May and September. A winter there would surely be an experience.

So, late in October, after a fortnight in Edinburgh of goodbyes, good lucks and a good many offers to come and see us on the island (little did we know), we crossed from Stranraer to Belfast and headed for Strangford Lough like the two old sea dogs we definitely were not. I say 'were' advisedly – we may be now.

It had been three years since our last brief visit and after the traumas of recent weeks, we arrived at the yacht club pontoons as full-time residents feeling excited but fragile, unsure what was ahead. We backed the van down the concrete slipway almost to the water, intending to take a few boxes over in the dinghy and see about getting some help (and a bigger boat) for the rest of our stuff the following day. Back up the slipway I spotted John Scott, only partially visible in red oilskins behind the curtain of spray from a pressure hose, and wandered across the boat park to ask him whether his father's boat *Horsa* might be available next day.

This late in the season, many of the yachts had come off their summer moorings and stood side by side on trailers in the parking area. They looked vaguely embarrassed, their underpants ignominiously exposed to the world. One called *Syrena*, whose lines in the water might have broken hearts, had just been dragged out of her natural habitat by, of all things, a common agricultural tractor; and there she was, parked unceremoniously on the concrete apron while John used the pressure hose to remove slime, barnacles and weedy growth that had managed to get a hold below her water line. A steady stream of semi-coagulated green goo was running the length of her keel and cascading off its trailing edge at his feet. She reminded me of Jock, our Cairn, during one of his infrequent soapy ablutions under the garden hose back in Scotland: miserable, rigid, but unwaveringly stoical, too proud to make a scene. Pointedly, the terriers had disappeared together on urgent business to the far end of the pontoons just in case.

John Scott was a familiar face from as far back as I could remember. A shipwright and jack of all trades, he had been informally apprenticed to his legendary father, Bob, who over the years has turned his gifted hand to many things besides boats: scale models, carved figures and even gypsy caravans. John more or less took over when his father suffered a stroke in 1994, and is contracted by some of the owners to haul their boats out for the winter, handle running repairs and keep the moorings safe and in good order. He is also expected to deal with emergencies – boats aground, adrift or otherwise in trouble – and if it hadn't occurred to me before, it did now: uncertain of our new environment I would be grateful to have this obliging character around. A big man with a big smile, he laid down the hose, reached out his hand and managed to make us feel entirely welcome.

'Good to see you!' he said. 'Is this you then?'

'Just a look-see today. Any chance of some transport tomorrow for the rest of our stuff?'

I pointed to the van, grateful that he couldn't see from this angle that it was, can I say, fullish.

'No problem. Daddy and I will be here all day. Give me a shout when you're ready. Take the punt any time you need to get out to the boat.'

We took him at his word and I rowed his little double-ender out to collect the With. I admit I was keenly – blushingly – aware of his presence on the slip because only the day before, the With and I had had a character-building experience together from which I was still a little unnerved. It turns out that lots of things take some getting used to when it comes to actually living on an island, and nothing can be taken for granted, especially boats.

How much of what happened had registered with John, I can't say, but I was pretty sure he had been around. Suddenly I didn't want to catch his eye and as I rowed into the sound I looked over my shoulder more often than strictly necessary to check my direction, reliving the previous afternoon's events in a private haze of mortification. After some fibreglass repairs, a clean-up and a coat of anti-fouling, David and I had trailered the With down to Ringhaddy behind his Land Rover. We had no plans to cross to the island: the idea was simply to test the motor and leave the boat on the mooring. I walked alongside while David reversed the trailer down the slipway into the water. As soon as the boat began to float I gave her a shove and tied the bow rope to a cleat on the floating pontoon walkway. We manhandled the outboard out of the Land Rover and onto the transom, tightened it in position and connected the fuel line. All set, I squatted on the edge of the pontoon and held the boat in, motioning David onto the stern seat so that he could start the motor. He demurred and instead gave me a few tips on the foibles of this particular outboard: 'Start is up, not too much choke from cold ... be ready for her to start on the third pull ... above all hit the choke and take the revs off as soon as she even thinks of firing. Put her in gear and away you go.'

No problem. I could do all that. While David watched from the pontoon, I climbed in and planted one foot on the transom, bracing myself to pull the start cord. *Start is up, not too much choke from cold.* I pulled the choke three-quarters out, flicked up the red ignition switch. *She starts on the third pull.* Once, twice; away she went. Excellent. *Hit the choke as soon as she fires.* That one is tricky because you have to do it almost in one continuous movement otherwise the carburettor floods; but I managed it and felt, I don't mind saying, quite a bit pleased. *Put her in gear.* Still bent over the motor, I hesitated because there was just the hint of a niggle in the back of my mind. Oh well. I slid the lever towards me and it was as if forward gear and my brain engaged in the same instant.

Take the revs off! It was too late and the boat seemed to rear up and spin around and practically go airborne all at once. Flailing both arms in the direction of the tiller arm, I managed to get hold of the throttle control with my right – actually my wrong – hand and made things worse by turning the twist-grip towards 'fast', the only mitigating factor being that although I probably hit twenty knots from a standing start, I seemed by a happy chance to be in clear water and heading away from the pontoons in a wide and stylish circle. I'm not sure if I was more embarrassed or terrified. Embarrassed, I think. I was acutely aware, even *in medio periculo*, that David was watching while I tried to wreck his boat, the outboard, and whichever expensive yacht I was fated to make contact with first. I have an image of him in my mind's eye, frozen there for ever, and he isn't bawling instructions at his stupid incompetent idiot little brother, shaking his head in disbelief or even running for his life up the pontoons. He's just standing there as cool as you like with his eyes half-closed and the trace of a smile on his lips, a picture of brotherly forbearance – bless him.

Hammering thus unexpectedly around the anchorage, a white and orange blur of mooring buoys and yachts flashing by on either side, I tried to command my offending right hand to turn in exactly the opposite direction to that dictated by instinct. It was like trying to rub my tummy and pat my head at the same time, something I was never very good at. With only a subtle change of course I would fly – almost literally – past the cruising club's 'MAXIMUM SPEED IN THE SOUND: 5 KNOTS' floating admonition in a few more seconds, and then I would be out of the confines of the anchorage and speeding north, where the next stop might be the wide expanses of tidal mud flats covering the extreme northern end of the lough five miles away. With a world reputation for wading birds, but much too shallow for anything drawing more water than a duck, I might not encounter much up there in the way of shipping hazards but a few thousand redshank would certainly stop what they were doing and stare in my direction if I ploughed a V-shaped furrow across the surface of their vast and pristine dining table.

Whether by trial and error or force of David's concentrated will, I managed to throttle down as the With was coming to the end of her first complete circle and we crashed obliquely onto the edge of the pontoons, skidding along the timber scuffboard with a prolonged and teeth-clenching squeal and finally coming to a bobbing, smoking stop just eight or ten yards along from where we started. As the motor settled into the modulated *putt-putt* of a quiet and healthy tick-over, I tried to tell myself it had all been a worthwhile, even essential, part of the learning curve, like falling off Joey aged six and a half with my foot still caught in the stirrup.

When David stepped into the boat as if nothing had happened, we went for a sedate and dignified cruise of the vicinity to satisfy ourselves that all was well. Not a word was spoken between us, and if a small crowd had joined John in the boat park, we didn't notice because we were not looking in that direction. Besides, if anyone *had* been watching, I knew I could handle it: 'Been around boats half my life. You think I didn't mean to do that?'

Six

I confess that the following day, when I left Lynn sorting boxes on the slipway and rowed up alongside the With in John's punt, I was careful to rehearse the starting procedures in my mind.

I tied the punt to the stern of the With and climbed aboard; started the outboard without any trouble and made my way forward to untie the bow rope from the mooring buoy. With both boats free to move in the current, I made my way back to the outboard as swiftly as my land legs would allow, stepping over the two seats, an anchor and the fuel tank and keeping a hand on the gunwale for balance. I sat down, took the twist-grip in my left – my *left* – hand and leaned over the outboard to pull the gear lever forward. The propeller bit and I motored slowly ahead, whistling softly; projecting, I hope, an air of quiet professionalism.

After returning the punt to the pontoon and shouting my thanks to John, I rejoined Lynn and we began loading boxes onto the dinghy. When we realised, after half an hour, that the amount of freeboard was beginning to look marginal and the exact position of each additional box was, in terms of stability, becoming critical, we called it a day and left the rest in the van.

We parked up and called for the dogs. Rab, the Westie, hirpled along the foreshore towards us with his usual disorganised gait, wagging his tail propeller-style. Jock followed at a respectable distance, his more leisurely pace reflecting his years and a strong notion that too swift a reaction in Cairns can seem like an abrogation of the independence to which the breed is born. Lynn jumped down to the shingle and lifted Rab onto the pontoon, but thought better of doing the same for Jock. Instead, she jogged back up the foreshore, calling for him to follow, and led him onto the pontoon via the ramp at the end.

It has been the cause of some angst and a great many embarrassing moments for Lynn and me over the years that despite having lived together since they were pups, the two dogs have never fully accommodated one another and will occasionally fight, as they say, like terriers. We know all the flash points and try to avoid them: lifting Jock when Rab is anywhere near is one. As soon as he sees that Jock's paws have left the ground, Rab manoeuvres himself with mischievous intent to exactly the spot at which he anticipates their return. Jock knows this from long experience and views Rab's behaviour as a kind of death wish, a gratuitous invasion of personal space that cannot be tolerated. The moment we stoop to lift him he turns rigid as a log, fixes an eye on Rab and lets rip with the kind of bloodcurdling growls and snapping of jaws that have passers-by staring at us with expressions of shock and contempt. While one of us grabs Rab and holds him back, the other lowers Jock to the ground and holds *him* back; the only problem being that another flash point is when we hold either of them back.

You can't win, at least not all the time, and the only consolation is that as these two late middle-aged – geriatric really – characters get stiffer and lazier their gladiatorial encounters are becoming quite rare and it's noticeable that when they dust themselves down and hobble away afterwards, they tend to leave less blood on the walls and floor.

We walked along the pontoon to the point where it began to float, and as soon as Rab felt the ground move beneath his feet he stopped dead and did the splits, flattening his stomach against the concrete. He does the same in lifts when we press 'Down'; his claws dig deep into the carpet, his eyes go left and right and his expression says 'What the …?' as if it's the first time it has ever happened. With a little reassurance, alarm normally turns to mild suspicion and he's willing to pick himself up, but since that first occasion he has never quite got used to the pontoons and on a stormy day, when they buck and creak with the waves and salty spray leaves a swirling layer of foam underfoot, he has been known to do an infantry crawl the entire length of the walkway, pausing every so often before darting forward in a sniper-foiling zigzag, finally reaching the boat in a panting, tail-wagging delirium of pride and relief.

Before getting into the boat, Lynn and I stood together on the pontoon for a moment and looked diagonally off to the right in the direction of the cabin half a mile away – an indistinct blue sliver against the bulk of Islandmore. For sure this was an important moment for us. We were about to open a new door with only the vaguest idea of what lay behind it. I said, 'After you', and Lynn took my hand and stepped carefully down into the boat. Rab sat alert and upright in her lap, and Jock stood beside her on the mahogany seat. I pulled the dinghy along the pontoon towards deeper water, pushed off and stepped down onto the stern seat behind them.

The crossing itself was straightforward, perhaps even auspicious. The day was fresh and bright and an uncertain breeze was airbrushing shadowy, haphazard ripples onto the sound. Even so, when I felt the water touch my fingertips where they rested on the gunwale – a good foot above what would normally be the water line – I succumbed to a wimpish urge to keep, as our seaman friend, Jim, would say, 'a grip of the land', and made a dog-leg of the short journey to the cabin, heading straight across the sound before turning south and hugging the west side of the island, with the outboard barely above tick-over.

The overladen With behaved impeccably, only once wallowing ever so slightly when Jock moved along the seat to plant his front paws on the gunwale and peer over the side. Grateful that eleven years earlier we had gone for terriers and not labradors, I motioned Lynn to shift an inch or two in the opposite direction. Perfect. We chose our line between the moorings and had time to admire at close quarters the cormorants standing sentinel on every second or third buoy. Broken sunlight bounced off the water and picked up the bronzes and greens of their autumn plumage, indiscernible at a distance, and one or two held their oil-less wings outstretched and faced the sun to dry, proud and statuesque, the living maritime equivalent of the gold-leaf gatepost eagles of suburbia.

As we puttered along the island shoreline the cabin began to come into view ahead of us and to the left: first the very tips of the few remaining Scots pines from the scores planted eighty years ago to take the brunt of a northerly wind, then the wooden jetty dipping out into the water towards the mainland, and finally the cabin itself. It huddles in the lee of Eagle Hill, protected from the prevailing southwesterlies by the motherly arm of her southern slope where it sweeps down to the water to guard the entrance to the sound; and it is, to my way of thinking, the ultimate waterfront cabin, the very sum and essence of the type: long and low, stilted to the front, downhill side, felt-roofed and weather-boarded, with multi-paned windows on the seaward side and a halfdoor in the middle. Larger rooms project forward from either end and a wide timber veranda runs the length of the house between them. Nothing is quite square. The ridgeline of the black roof sags into a row of gentle smiles and at various points the cabin has settled so erratically on its timber piers that windows refuse to meet within rhomboid frames and only in one room – happily the living room – is it possible to walk on the level.

Two sets of steep wooden steps drop down to the grass from opposite ends of the veranda, and at high tide it is just six paces from the bottom step to the water. Sitting out on the veranda when the tide is up, you feel as though you could go to the edge, poke your legs through the timber balustrade and dangle your feet in the water, and at certain times of the year, when exceptionally high tides and westerly gales coincide, you probably could, though it might not be much fun.

Once, after a particularly ferocious January storm, the retreating tide left behind a line of foamy seaweed on the grass, which touched the base of the deck supports, and we began to see why the cabin had been built on stilts in the first place. That was a pretty high tide on a three-quarter moon, but the mind boggles at what might happen if a westerly force ten and a big tide were ever to arrive together. Simon, one of our more romantic visitors, intrigued by the notion that from the inside, with the muffled *thump-thump* of the generator in the background, the cabin feels for all the world like a Mississippi paddle steamer, willed the view to change before his first visit to the window each day and might have been truly impressed to discover one morning that it really had. At the whim of wind and tide, the cabin could end up anywhere; potentially, I suppose, at the far southern end of the lough, bobbing along at eight knots towards the open sea and pausing to pirouette once or twice in the larger whirlpools that fringe the angry waters of the Narrows. Our options for doing anything about it being limited, we could at least take our toast and coffee onto the veranda to enjoy the changing view, and with any luck the Portaferry lifeboat would be called out by some sympathetic yachtsman bemused to sight an apparently skipperless house adrift and out of control on the water.

I glanced back towards the mainland and John gave a wave from the boat park. I wondered aloud if he had witnessed yesterday's shenanigans with the With, and in the same breath wondered who I was kidding. He hadn't mentioned it, but that didn't mean he was deaf and blind.

turquoise boat. yellow man

Seven

Fortunately, apart from the cormorants, there was no one to witness our actual arrival. Without labouring the details, which had to do with excess weight, forward momentum and a pleasant rediscovery of my childhood interest in bird-watching, we stopped more suddenly than intended when the bow met the jetty, and a cardboard box decorated with felt-tip sketches of kitchen sundries, including, ominously, a cup and saucer, which had been balanced optimistically across the bow, ended up teetering half on and half off the jetty, unsure whether to stick with it or try to return to the boat. Thankfully it went for the jetty in the end because the boat had bounced back and wasn't there any more. I cut the motor and we drifted with the current away from the clear water beside the jetty and into the tangle of seaweed to the side, grabbed an oar each and poled our way back, gondolier-style.

The plank footway of the jetty rests on uprights made from old railway sleepers and runs at chest height from the top of a retaining sea wall in front of the cabin to just beyond the low-water mark, seventy yards or so into the sound. With care, it's wide enough for two people to pass each other, and the footing is sound when it's dry and clean, but it does present a challenge to the dogs. A five-lane aerial highway with barnacle-fringed gaps between the planks to discourage lane changes, its seaward end, underwater for most of the tidal cycle, is apt to collect a treacherous veneer of slimy sediment and weed and the dogs have learned that once committed to a particular plank it's wise to stay with it.

Even when, psychologically constrained in this way, they find themselves travelling in opposite directions on the same plank and meet face to face, rather than risk a lane change or some kind of aerial confrontation, the one nearest to terra firma will make a slow and deliberate U-turn, placing each paw with great delicacy and retracing his steps as far as the grassy strip between the top of the jetty and the cabin.

We left everything where it was and the four of us walked gingerly up the jetty in single file, climbed the steps to the veranda and opened the front door. A rush of salt, wood-scented air met us, the perfume of sea and civilisation come together; of paraffin oil and damp canvas; turf smoke, timber and old books. Inside, the panelled corridor that fronts the cabin was filled with the paraphernalia of frenetic family weekends and hasty Sunday evening departures. A dinghy boom with furled sail hung from rusty cup-hooks between two of the bedroom doors. Folding tables, deck chairs and three-legged stools were stacked against the walls. A collection of lamps – Tilleys, storm lanterns and a blackened brass Victorian mantel lamp – were lined up on either side of a framed collage of family snapshots on a long shelf that ran below the windows.

Some of this stuff took me back to the seventies. My first pair of binoculars still hung beside the door. They were given me by my grandparents when I came across the leather case in their glory hole, the name they gave to an attic space that was the final resting place for the First of everything – an enormous first-generation Teasmade, miniature cameras and miscellaneous gadgetry, all bought on impulse by Grandfather to be used only once or not at all before being consigned to the glory hole by my grandmother. The binoculars were already old when I found them, and although they had a focusing ring that worked in an approximate kind of way, there was no means of adjusting the width to suit my eyes and on my early bird-watching expeditions I used to hold one side with both hands and use the other as a kind of monocular. Even today I find them frustratingly wide and if the gap between our eyes really does have something to do with honesty, they must have been designed for someone unable to tell a lie.

That wouldn't be me. When my parents gave me my first penknife on the morning of my sixth birthday, I ran outside to do stuff with it and managed to cut my thumb almost to the bone before I'd got as far as the stable yard. Convinced I was about to lose the knife for ever, or at least that it would languish in the back of a drawer until I reached my seventh birthday, and adulthood, I tried to persuade my mother that when I ran my hand along the harled wall of one of the stables, I had encountered a very, very sharp stone. I must thank her because she didn't call my bluff or scold me, she just made sympathetic noises and whisked me off, bleeding profusely, to the bathroom and the first-aid box.

Lynn and I made our way along the corridor, opening each bedroom door in turn and peering inside. The three smaller ones, facing east and denied the sun's heat by the steep bank at the back of the cabin, felt chill and a little damp. I paused in the third – my own room as a child – and smiled because so little had changed. The same broken trout rod poked out from under the steel bed and the same two posters were pinned to the wall. One was a mariner's wall chart with maps of epic sea voyages, cut-away line drawings of square-riggers, whalers and warships and, my favourite always, a panel showing a variety of knots with wild and romantic names like Turk's-head, sheepshank, stevedore's, and the ubiquitous, universal and what-on-earth-did-they-do-before-it-was-invented bowline and all its subtle variants – Portuguese bowline, double bowline, water bowline, Spanish bowline, bowline on the bight. Wonderful.

The other poster was a little surreal, a shimmering, mind-bending arrangement of concentric circles in bright red on a blue ground with, at its epicentre, the single word 'NOW' in big red capitals. What it said to me as a dreamy, introverted adolescent I can't think and possibly it would have been more apropos on the wall of my office in later years as a permanent, finger-pointing admonition aimed at the serial procrastinator I had become: 'NOW would be a good time to get the records out of the shoebox and into the computer.'

An estate agent would describe the main bedroom, which is the full depth of the cabin and opens off the end of the corridor, as flooded with light and having a spectacular west-facing French window giving onto the timber veranda, with open views across the sound; and as regards sunlight, orientation and aspect, that would be a fair enough description. 'French window', though, would be going a bit far, as it simply happens that one of the windows is low enough to give access to the veranda outside as long as you're careful not to trip over the sill or bump your head on the lintel as you go. It provides a short cut through the bedroom towards the bathroom, which in turn can only be reached from the veranda. Our friend John Shaw christened it the Inland Route and Lynn habitually, and in all seriousness, invites visitors to use it on rainy nights as an alternative to a refreshing dash along the veranda from the front door to the – admittedly only – toilet. It's an invitation I have harboured doubts about since she first issued it, and no one, I'm glad to say, has so far taken it up, at least not in the middle of the night.

On a wall-mounted shelf beside the bed there was a new-looking engineer's vice and a large blue-painted biscuit tin, from which a length of fishing line hung down in spirals almost to the floor. I sat on the bed and pulled the box down onto my lap. The contents had my brother written all over them: a nautical almanac from 1994; a plastic container with little compartments for weights and mackerel lures; a can of oil and some tools; a length of multicoloured nylon rope.

Lynn was looking over my shoulder and I noticed she had gone quiet. I put the box back and we walked to the living room at the far end of the cabin. Everything there – the board games and old yachting magazines crammed onto the shelves, the Admiralty charts of Strangford and the west coast of Scotland on the walls, the eclectic mix of cushions, throws and mismatched furniture – it all said the same thing and I began to see what was troubling her. The cabin had been so much a part of other people's lives that we felt like intruders, without any real right to be there: not, at any rate, to live there.

Although it belonged to my mother, the cabin's use, enjoyment and maintenance, given that I had been living in Scotland and Claire was more interested in horses than in boats, had fallen by default to David and his wife, Gail. Over the years, while their children were growing up, they had spent summer holidays and countless weekends on the island. David kept a yacht moored in the sound, just off the end of the jetty. When the generator, the roof or the jetty required repair, the responsibility, and the cost, fell on him. Everywhere we looked we saw their belongings and felt their presence, and generous as they had been when we first raised the idea of coming to live on the island, it came home to us then that they would be giving up something special in their lives just for us, and we were not at all sure we deserved it.

Lynn perched on the edge of the window seat with her back to one of the prettiest views in County Down. She frowned and shook her head slowly, studying the floor.

'It feels wrong,' she said.

I understood, but it was different for me. David was my brother and if someone was to be displaced, better that it was family, and for the right reasons. From when we were old enough to understand, our parents instilled in all of us their own 'pull together' family ethos, which rightly or wrongly I have always taken for granted; certainly, this was not the time to question it. We were where we were. And David and Gail had been at pains to reassure us that with other commitments their visits to the island had in any case become sporadic in recent years. Obviously I was more able than Lynn to take that at face value, so it would be up to me to convince her that if her in-laws found themselves in a position to help us out, it would give them nothing but pleasure to do so. I told her something that my mother had said to me when we arrived in Ireland. Anxious not to embarrass Lynn by telling her directly, my mother wanted me to know that she saw her as a daughter and that there was nothing she would do for me that she wouldn't equally have done for Lynn.

'I know that,' Lynn said. 'I hope she realises it's mutual.'

We talked, and in few words fell back on the ultimate given, repeated so often it had become a kind of mantra – that come what may, we would have each other and could move forward together.

Through the window behind her, towards the west and the mainland, I became aware that dramatic transformations were taking place in the sound, as though virtual stagehands were labouring to effect a grand and atmospheric set change before my very eyes, a day's end flourish with which to wow their audience of newcomers; and it struck me that there were compensations to quitting the rat race after all, and that the most impressive one was all around us.

'Wow,' I said.

Clearly it was a day for defining moments, because when Lynn turned to look, her whole manner appeared to turn too, as though breathing it all in made her stronger, more resolved. A timely appeal to her sense of aesthetics, the spectacle seemed to render her just as speechless as me, and like me, she plumbed the depths of her word well for a fitting reaction.

'Wow!' she said.

For a minute or two we just stared. With dusk approaching, it had become very still on the sound. From behind the wooded hills on the far shore a lambent sunset blush had begun to spread upwards, touching the clouds' under edges and laying a reddening cast on the water. Silhouetted black against the lough, the kiltered steel pole, which announces the end of the jetty to incautious helmsmen, rose like Excalibur from the water and thrust its cuneate head to the sky, and the promise of infinite possibilities.

After a few moments, Lynn slapped her hands down onto her knees and stood up. 'Well ...' she said; and I knew from her tone of voice that the matter had been put to bed and that it was time to get on.

Lynn doesn't linger, brood or get uptight the way I do, preferring to rely on a chain-mail of sang-froid through which raw emotion is only rarely visible, and then generally to me alone. I used to wonder what the trick was. Given to fairly frequent episodes of self-pity, moodiness and even, embarrassingly enough, the odd temper tantrum myself, I couldn't at first see where she put it all. But if you look closely, it's there in her paintings: the charge, the passion and the vulnerabilities of one of the most well-rounded and empathetic people I know.

Just occasionally I have had the opportunity, when I felt I wasn't distracting her, to watch as Lynn worked through the creative process in her studio, and it's an absorbing, dare I say, exhausting business. She lays her board on the floor so that she can assess it from all angles while she works it up. Almost absently at first, she stands away, mixes colours, makes a mark or two. Then she eyes the board with something between nurture and fascination until its direction and final orientation begin tentatively to suggest themselves to her subconscious. Eventually she becomes transfixed, wholly focused, and hovers over the painting like a swordsman determined to deliver the *coup de grâce* on a downed but worthy opponent who is unwilling to submit. On some undiscoverable impulse – to mortals anyway – she lunges repeatedly forward and downward, making gestural but precise brushstrokes – *thrust, feint, parry, riposte* – until the suggestion of a mood or atmosphere, encapsulating the spirit of a particular landscape at a particular moment, begins to emerge, as if by – I don't know, by force of will or sleight of hand. It beats me.

It can take an hour or a day or many days, and the final piece may not stand re-examination even a short time after completion, finding itself consigned to oblivion with a ruthlessness that ensures, like natural selection, that only the best survive and that, little by little, the quality of the work will always improve. Whether it survives or not, though, the cathartic release that accompanies the whole process seems to be as lifeblood to Lynn, as presumably to many artists.

Among those few of Lynn's paintings we have kept for ourselves, my particular favourite is a large landscape overlaid with a rare self-portrait in charcoal. The piece says a great deal about the context in which Lynn sees herself – the landscape is literally seen *through* the figure – and while it captures much of her beauty, it also has the intensity, the frowning concentration, that distinguishes so many self-portraits and seems to give them an edge. I love that when I look at the painting, she seems to be giving me her undivided attention – sharing a confidence perhaps. Lynn would never hang it – she has moved on and in any case tends not to hang her own work – and that gives me the extra satisfaction of exclusivity. This particular McGregor (Lynn paints under her maiden name) will never leave the house.

For 'work' read 'life'. Lynn has much the same approach to both; that's to say, she hits them head on and relishes a challenge. If resolve had momentarily given way to apprehension when we first walked into the house, it wasn't for very long, because before I could say, 'Which box is the coffee in?' she had rolled up her sleeves and begun lugging them from the boat up to the cabin.

We crossed paths at the top of the jetty and I could see she was giving the cabin the kind of look she normally reserves for blank boards on the studio floor: more appraisal, thank goodness, than apprehension. The cabin was about to be 'Lynn'd', and three weeks, a good deal of paint, some weathered and abandoned timber from a local builder's yard and thirty or forty empty boxes later, she was able to put one particular demon to rest when Gail, on her first visit to the island since our move, opened the front door, smiled with evident approval and said: 'Ahh ... Quilchena-on-Sea!'

Eight

My journal entry for 12 November, brief and only mildly encoded with the usual obscure references and *aides-mémoire*, reads: 'Sunny. Wind light SW. Breakfast on the veranda. Bob & John loaned *Horsa* to ferry rest of stuff. Lynn's throne. (Cleopatra) No generator! *Quiet* night …'

'Cleopatra' has to do with the stately splendour in which Lynn made the crossing aboard *Horsa* the following day, in company with the heavier and more awkward items, which we had left on the mainland and which might have tested the With's lateral stability to the limits, certainly to the other side of good sense. Finding herself trapped between one end of a rustic garden seat, which we placed across *Horsa*'s raised foredeck, and a sheer drop to the water, and unable to regain the pontoon without clambering over yet more boxes, she took the opportunity to recline where she was, and luckily for her, resisted any temptation to torment her toiling minions by directing final loading and embarkation operations with little movements of her wrist and fingers.

Horsa has been so much a part of the fabric of life on Ringhaddy Sound during forty years that she has become a kind of talisman to many who sail these waters. Imbued with the spirit, as it were, of the lough itself – beautiful, timeless and somehow warmly reassuring – she was originally commissioned as a lifeboat aboard one of a pair of sister North Sea ferries named *Hengist* and *Horsa* before the Second World War. Both ferries were commandeered as troop carriers and *Horsa* saw action, and no doubt saved lives, when her namesake was torpedoed and sunk in 1942. Double-ended, clinker-built larch on oak and powered by a twin-cylinder Lister engine, the understated elegance of her lines, even to the uninitiated, suggests something of the workmanlike ease with which she moves in the water: a perfect marriage, if ever there was one, of form and function.

Of all the images I associate with the island, her classic silhouette as she passes by the cabin on a summer's evening will probably be the most enduring. In my mind's eye Bob Scott stands square at the tiller and gazes fixedly ahead, a pipe between his teeth, motionless but for the occasional lift of his hand to acknowledge the salute of another boat out on the water.

Needless to say, with John at the helm, the business of coming alongside the jetty was accomplished with an inspirational blend of verve and aplomb. While John was chatting to Lynn and me, his hand was moving smoothly between *Horsa*'s gear and throttle levers; and while I was saying how grateful we were for his help, a voice inside my head was saying, Watch and learn, son! Granted, it had not been her fault; but whereas the With had introduced herself to the jetty the day before with a gratuitous head butt, *Horsa* characteristically opted for a gentle kiss on the cheek instead.

I mentioned that Bob Scott is something of a legend in these parts. Well into his eighties, he is the living embodiment of a much-advocated and rarely practised ideal: that even with advancing years and failing health it shouldn't be a question of how much you can still do, but how slowly you can countenance doing it. Bob is persistently, incorrigibly and, it has to be said, sometimes recklessly active and he certainly doesn't look his age. He is wiry and straight and his dark, weather-worn features soften frequently into a youthful grin. In his long life he has been shipwright, fisherman, joiner and wood carver. From years of working with tools his hands are broad but his fingers have an eloquent fineness, suggesting both artisan and artist. He habitually wears a denim jacket and an old paint-spattered blue and white cap with soft badged crown and leather peak.

The quintessential man of the sea, Bob has lived as long as I can remember in a cottage by the sound. Everyone knows that he and *Horsa* have shared adventures of the kind the rest of us would call Once in a Lifetime, but I don't think I've had any of them from the

horse's mouth. It's not just that Bob is self-effacing. He genuinely doesn't see anything remarkable about his exploits, their being, as he would see it, merely part of getting the job done. It's left to others to tell his stories, and typically they begin, 'Bob? I'll never forget the time ...'

A few years ago, when Bob was still in his seventies, John noticed that his father's arm was bruised and swollen from wrist to elbow. He asked him about it and it turned out that the previous week, Bob had set out late in the evening to check his equipment on the far side of the lough. The night was blustery and moonless and as he finished up and turned for home his propeller caught a rope and became snagged. Not being very far from shore, he did have options, like waiting for daylight the better to assess things; but that would be the easy way. Instead, Bob grabbed a rusty hacksaw from under the foredeck; stripped, and lowered himself over the side of the boat. He was vague about how long afterwards, tired, cold and badly bruised from sawing and hacking so close to the propeller blade in the darkness, he climbed back aboard *Horsa*, put on his clothes and headed home to

Ringhaddy. Even his wife Annie didn't know about it. If John hadn't seen his arm, nobody would.

When John first told me the story, I wondered idly how many close calls his father might have had over the years; which was a bit like idly fingering the lid to Pandora's box.

'Where,' John said, 'would you start?'

Late on a stormy night in February 1990, Bob's friend Hans Carse, checking that all was well with his own boat, noticed Bob's was off her mooring. He used a torch to look up and down the sound and saw her in the shallows north of the quay. It was blowing a gale so he rushed to Bob's cottage and woke him by knocking on his bedroom window. The two of them set off along the foreshore and found that the boat was well aground. There was nothing they could do from the shore, but the tide was rising and Bob came up with a plan: he knew that there was a mooring buoy with a ring not far out into the sound, and that if a line could be run from the boat to the buoy, they could use the incoming tide to refloat her. He headed off to fetch a rope and his dinghy, refusing Hans's offer to go with him – quite possibly, in the process, saving his friend's life.

Hans waited on the foreshore, with instructions to shine his torch on the buoy, and presently Bob appeared in the rowing boat, pitching and bucking down the sound. As it came level with the buoy, the dinghy was caught by a gust and overturned. Bob disappeared, and as minutes went by, Hans understandably thought it was all over. He could see the upturned hull, but no Bob. Then, as the little boat came in to the shallows and Hans waded out to grab it, Bob stepped out from underneath, coughing seawater but otherwise none the worse. He had surfaced under the upturned hull and had the presence of mind to stay there, wrapping his legs around the seat and making use of the air pocket made famous by Hollywood. In real life most of us prefer to panic, but Bob is made of sterner stuff. Knowing that, given the direction of tide and wind, he was bound to fetch up somewhere along that stretch of shore, he simply waited. Rather him than me.

More recent, and of a different but equally impressive order of heroism, was Bob's relentless search for his missing pet goose. The entire neighbourhood was alerted: she had last been seen waddling along the path behind Bob's house and down the yacht club slipway into the water, where she had turned south. Unfortunately Lynn and

I weren't told about it until the following day, otherwise we might have intercepted her as she swam past the cabin.

Bob himself didn't know the goose was missing until later the same evening, by which time it was too late to give chase; but he took to the rowing boat anyway, returning empty-handed well after dark. He blamed himself for not shutting her in, as he normally would, after feeding, and at first light he was on the water again. We watched him row down the far side of the sound, hugging the shore, covering every inch of every bay, stopping at intervals to whistle. He was convinced she would come to him when she heard him, and he was probably right: we all knew there was a special bond between them. But despite a marathon row that lasted all day and took him round the entire circumference of both Islandmore and little Pawle Island, our neighbour to the southeast, he couldn't find her.

Next morning we took the With and joined the search – more, frankly, to keep an eye on Bob than with any hope of success – and this pattern was repeated, and the search area widened, over the following several days. We could only marvel at the stamina and single-mindedness that drove Bob to keep looking, but after a week even he was becoming reconciled to losing his goose, at least for the time being, and the rowing boat finally remained tied to the pontoons.

Bob continued to take for granted that one day the goose would come home, and happily three weeks later she did. She was picked up from the side of the road not far away, and taken to Castle Espie Wildfowl and Wetlands Centre, on the shores of the lough further north. There, a sharp-eyed member of staff, picking up on her unique distinguishing features – she was blind in one eye and had a nasty limp – said, 'Isn't that Bob's goose?'

Apparently when they went to collect her, she sat on Bob's lap in the car and made a noisy, resentment-fuelled fuss over him all the way home.

Bob clearly has a way with geese and the following story, coming from anyone other than the man himself, might have been apocryphal.

Many years ago, one of his geese died and the she-goose remaining was, he thought, in a broody state of mind. Resolved to help her out, he visited the nest of a Canada goose on one of the islands and selected an egg. It was well on, because before he could get it home it began to hatch, and the gosling's first awareness of the world was from inside the folds of Bob's denim jacket.

The incubator Bob had made up from a cardboard box, a light bulb and some straw was used, instead, as a nursery, and the youngster thrived. A gander, as he reached maturity he was nevertheless more interested in Bob, his only known parent, than in Bob's she-goose. The two of them used to watch television together; the goose would stand on the arm of Bob's chair and nibble his ear. When Bob left the house by car, the goose sometimes left too, flying along the shore wall at the level of the driver's window; several times, Bob had to put him in the car and take him home.

This very handsome bird continued to live as one of the family. Every morning he would fly across the sound to graze with a feral flock on Islandmore, and every evening Bob would whistle him in from the end of the quay. He would re-cross the sound and land at Bob's feet, and after a good feed, he would be closed in for the night – a mutually satisfactory arrangement that lasted for several seasons.

Then one autumn afternoon a large flock of his wilder cousins landed on the hillside across the road from the house, and began to graze. He showed some interest, but he stayed at home. They kept coming back, each time a little closer to the house, daring him to join them. One day he did, and that was that: when Bob whistled from the quay that night, he whistled to himself.

Come spring, Bob was working in his back yard one morning when a flight of Canada geese came up over the sound from the south.

As they passed by the old quay, a single bird separated from the rest, circled twice above his head, and followed the flock north.

In the person of Bob Scott, romance and reality seem to meet.

By the time Bob and John and I had ferried Cleopatra to her new island home and finished unloading *Horsa*, the jetty was stacked two-deep with boxes, from the water line up to the front gate.

Lynn and I watched as *Horsa* disappeared in the direction of the yacht club, her engine note rising in pitch, becoming thinner, and finally fading altogether, leaving behind just the whisper-in-waiting of her wash's widening chevron of tiny wavelets. As one by one they came ashore and broke in a rhythmic series of little swishes that followed her up the sound, we stood for a long time in the silence they left behind. I put an arm around Lynn's shoulders and I could feel that she was beginning to relax.

She took a deep breath of island air and allowed herself, hopefully, the luxury of a small foretaste of its calming and restorative magic.

Nine

Darkness was almost upon us, so as a cowhand friend used to say, we had to hang and rattle. I never did find out where that expression came from and I never heard anyone else use it, but every morning through the branding season on the ranch, when we were required to be saddled and ready to ride out by 5 a.m., Louis Denver would wake first, tiptoe across the bunkhouse in his long johns and open the front door without making a sound. Then he would slam it shut and yell, 'Ay-o-coffaayo!' (tea or coffee?) and 'Let's hang and rattle, boys!' I was young and a green horse and tumbled out of bed in stunned obedience, but the others used to throw boots at him.

Lynn and I settled on my old bedroom as a storage and distribution point and before long it was gutted and lined on three sides with boxes. In a way it became our very own glory hole because every so often while we rushed about, one of those felt-tip sketches would tug at our heart strings with extra persistence and we would rummage for something special, which having survived a brutal filtering operation in Scotland a month or two earlier, really meant something to us: a framed photo of Lynn and her father laughing together in the garden at Quilchena; the Zuñi fetish – a pair of carved stone wolves – which we gave to each other on our tenth wedding anniversary. Bound together with sinew and decorated with pieces of New Mexican turquoise, the wolves now stand, their heads inclined towards one another so they almost touch, on a piece of flat-topped driftwood that serves as a shelf on the wall of the cabin living room.

At one point, as I was passing the bedroom door, I caught Lynn staring with a pained expression at my NOW poster, and became suspicious. She may have taken my look to be one of lingering farewell because she said mildly: 'So. Can I throw this out now?'

'No.'

'How about *NOW*?'

I wasn't about to concede, but I could put my foot down and still have no way of knowing what she might do when my back was turned.

I said, 'If anyone's going to throw it out, it ought to be me', and I began to unpin it from the wall, very slowly in the manner of a child told to tidy his room.

Lynn gave me an old-fashioned look, but all credit to her, she did leave me to it. I rolled the poster up tightly and for some weeks it was moved through a series of ingenious hiding places, finally ending up when the dust had settled in one of the spare bedrooms, tight against the back wall under the bed where Lynn was unlikely to find it, in company of the said broken trout rod, which curiously enough I also discovered to be under threat.

In near darkness, while Lynn tackled the wood burner in the living room, I lined up some oil lamps on the veranda and topped them up

with paraffin. They were ancient and a bit smoky but they were all we had, and I distributed them through kitchen, corridor and living room. For sentimental reasons, I also hung one on a wooden bracket outside the front door.

As a twelve-year-old with a taste for the dramatic, I recall waiting late one summer's night for my father to come home. It was blowing a gale and we hung a Tilley lantern, hissing and spluttering and swinging wildly in the wind, as a beacon to guide him in to the jetty. In foul weather he always wore a full-length double-breasted black oilskin coat and a skipper's peaked cap, and I can still see him more or less falling through the front door and slamming it shut behind him against the driving rain. Water ran off his coat as he stood in the candlelight of the corridor, grinning and rubbing his hands together, and a black puddle grew at his feet as we gathered up to hear his news.

My father only ever seemed to manage a day or two of uninterrupted family time before his presence, or perhaps comment, was urgently required on the mainland, following political developments or the latest terrorist outrage; and before a guard hut was established on the island, complete with two-way radio, his office relied on a rudimentary system of signals to attract his attention.

Bob Dougal had a flagpole in the garden of his cottage at the quay. Someone at Stormont, normally my father's Private Secretary, Robert Ramsay, would telephone police headquarters in Belfast, who would radio the guard on the quay, who would ask Bob to raise the flag; and the height to which it was raised was meant to indicate the relative urgency of the call. During crisis-prone periods, which is to say more or less all the time, we got in the habit of periodically looking over toward Bob's. If the flag was flying, we would take a closer look with binoculars. I don't ever remember seeing anyone jump up and down or wave their arms in the air; the only discernible movement, aside from the flag, being the flapping tails of half a dozen identical grey overcoats lined up on the quay in expectation of my father's return. But duty having called, Da would disappear into the cabin to find a suit and his briefcase while we attempted to second-guess the situation on the mainland.

There is a squared hole in the forward thwart of the With where the mast would normally locate, but being seldom used, the mast was removed some years ago and lashed to a wooden fence in front of the cabin to serve as a flagpole. Bereft of an actual flag, it is mute and lifeless but I often think that had it been available to us back then, we might have managed a semblance of two-way communication – some means of registering a collective sigh. Three flag positions would amply have covered our usual responses: Low for 'Leave us alone'; half-mast for 'Can't it wait?'; and high for 'OK he's coming'.

Island days were always flatter when my father was called away, but at least it was in the nature of his absences that we could hope to track his movements by listening to the news.

On one of his late evening flag-alerts the message, when he got to the quay, was that he should telephone the office immediately. The nearest phone box was two miles away at the Toye. It's not there any more, which is a pity because there might still have been a London telephone number scratched on the glass in the minuscule script of my father's barely legible handwriting. By the time he arrived there it was dusk, and when he got through to the office, Robert gave him a Home Office number in London, which he was to call as a matter of urgency. He had no pen and in desperation he used his car keys to etch the number on the glass. History doesn't relate what the Home Secretary of the day wanted to talk to him about but the incident has always conjured for me the cosy, somewhat surreal, image of my father's diminutive figure dimly lit on that quiet County Down back road; of affairs of state conducted, so to speak, on the fly.

While I was footering with oil lamps, Lynn had managed to establish a roaring fire. In my role as hunter-provider, it's not easy for me to say this, but she does have a way with fires, an Apache touch which I don't pretend to understand. She talks about airflow and positioning but I think it goes deeper than that, otherwise I would be able to do it too. At Quilchena we had an open fire and when the wind was in the east, it had a tendency to die for lack of a good draw, leaving just a scattering of blackened, smoking logs and an apparently lifeless bed of grey ash. My first thought was always to start again, with newspapers and kindling, but Lynn could call back a flame using only the dying embers' glow, an artful rearrangement of the logs and two or three lungfuls of strangely inspirited air. Spooky.

With heat and light covered, the next thing on the list of priorities was our bed. Apart from a proprietorial pride in this, the signature piece of my erstwhile range of Santa Fe designs, the reason I wanted our own bed in place was that it has a solid base and a special mattress, a combination that has evolved over the years to provide my best chance of a reasonable sleep. As a student, I slipped a disc during a judo competition and despite the many kinds of surgical intervention to which I have been driven since – laminectomy, spinal fusion, lumber facet rhizotomy and various types of cordal block – I have never, like so many others, been able to shake off the pain, and my ability to function with any normality has to do with how much of it I am prepared to tolerate at the time.

Shortly after my injury, I consulted an orthopaedic surgeon in Aberdeenshire and in the vaguely patronising way peculiar to some people high up in the medical hierarchy, who seem to think that all their patients are between the ages of three and six, he explained that if my spine is a long train on a serpentine line, the last four carriages are poorly articulated – hence the pain shooting down my leg. Since then, and despite myself, I have visualised my pain as the tireless and demonic brakeman who stands at the very rear of the very last carriage, looking bleakly backwards and sending up showers of super-heated sparks around my lower back as he hauls remorselessly on the brake lever in an effort to slow me down, take me over – drive me on occasion, if the truth be told, almost off the rails.

I have consulted every kind of alternative therapist: osteopaths, chiropractors, acupuncturists, reflexologists, kinesiologists, hypnotists, homeopaths and healers – faith and otherwise. Most of them have been well intentioned but none of them, in my case at least, has been very effective. One or two, in fact, have been downright scary.

Once I was a quarter of an hour late for one of the ologists, I don't remember which, and when I arrived I apologised for keeping him. As I recall he was a small man, with bushy eyebrows and a deadpan expression.

'Fifteen minutes,' he said, 'is a long time when you're hanging by the neck. You are my sixth patient today and the others have all been on time. Please come with me.'

A little joke, I thought, but his expression clearly said, Think again.

I did please go with him but when we got as far as his consulting room, I panicked, apologised profusely (again) and fled. Poor man, he was probably fine; it may even have been a missed opportunity for me. But I had no wish to become his sixth victim of the day and as I limped with impolite haste towards my car, in my fancy I saw him standing in his consulting room, wild-eyed and trembling, ruing a missed opportunity of his own and eyeing the lever at the end of his black leather couch, and the telltale crack of the trap door in the floor beneath it.

The bed. Imaginatively named the 'Santa Fe', it has a heavy timber headboard panel framed between two posts, each inlaid with a fine band of Australian walnut harness leather. The panel is decorated with a row of carved Navajo wheat-sheaf motifs and the finish is a bleached woody grey, which imitates, as near as possible, the texture and tone of the kind of saltwater driftwood found on estuarine beaches at springtime.

The first proper piece of furniture from Quilchena to go into our new home, the bed was assembled in ten minutes and made us feel almost settled for the first time since leaving Scotland.

Finally the last box was off the jetty and squared away. We found the little rowing boat that belongs to the cabin upside down on its trolley, and hauled it from the grass bank beside the cabin, across the stones and down to the water's edge. Lynn went to see about something to eat while I took the two boats to David's mooring in the sound. By the time, in complete darkness, I had rather nervously tied the With to the mooring chain by means of a wholly unnecessary double bowline and two half-hitches, and rowed back to shore, the sweet smell of maple-cured bacon had drifted down the jetty to welcome me in. I tied up on the downwind side and made a note to look out the little fisherman's anchor from the shed later, so that I could fix a stern rope to the punt in case of a change of wind direction in the night; then strode up the jetty feeling fully the salt-blooded Captain Ahab of my boyhood fantasies, and threw open the door.

I said, 'Honey I be home. Aarr!' in a big deep voice.

Rab doesn't know how to handle funny voices, fearing, probably, that we have somehow mutated and become strangers. He flung himself at me, or pretended to, skidding to a stop just short of my ankles, growling, barking and wagging his entire hind end in a frenzy of conflicting emotions, as if to say, I love you! Don't take another step! It's so great to see you! Who are you?

I could see that Lynn was burning candles because a faint auroral flicker was coming from the archway into the kitchen. The smell was amazing: turf smoke was doing battle with the bacon, and beginning to win. We ate in front of the wood burner in the living room, and then settled down to read. To maximise light we sat together on the sofa and arranged the oil lamps in two little clusters, one on each side. I'm not sure who started it, but as the room slowly filled with acrid black smoke and our eyes began to stream, we got the giggles and were forced to abandon this first attempt at the simple life, and head for bed. Some of the lamps would have to go.

For a while we lay in the darkness thinking our own thoughts. Then Lynn said very quietly, 'Hard to believe.'

'What is?'

She propped herself on one elbow and I could tell she was looking out towards the water.

She said: 'The silence. The dark.'

I got up and stepped out through the bedroom window onto the veranda and stood at the rail. With a low moon over Eagle Hill, it was not, in fact, fully dark, but the silence was full-on. I listened hard. Not a thing.

It was my turn to take a deep breath. Already the island was getting under my skin and I was beginning to regain some sense of perspective: Willie Edgar would have been proud of me. Unlike the 'good' days when we thought we were rich but had no way of knowing what lay around the corner, we might now, relatively speaking, have nothing for the immediate future; but at least, as Lynn said, we would have control of nothing. It would be *our* nothing. No more the nightmare of depending on orders that didn't materialise, or the self-delusional bliss of five o'clock Friday afternoons when I knew that for a whole forty-eight hours the next telephone call would positively not be from the bank.

Here was an opportunity to take back our lives, and how often do you get to say that?

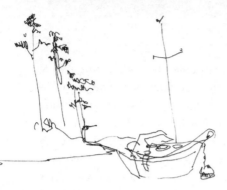

Ten

For a while the weather was unseasonably kind. The days were shortening, but while the sun shone and the nights were mild, we decided the house could wait. One practical worry, which lurked in the lean-to shed at the side of the cabin, I simply put to the back of my mind. The generator had refused to start on that first night. I did what I have always done – pressed the start button – and heard the faintest of clicks from inside the, um ... heard the faintest of clicks. Had he been there, my brother would have worked through his extensive repertoire of diagnostic procedures to isolate and fix the fault, but my own repertoire seems to begin and end with pressing the button and waiting for the lights to come on.

Hopeful of inspiration, or a sign, I stared hard at this colossal sixty-year-old machine with its belt-driven flywheels and its bank of batteries. Riveted onto a control box on the side, there was a worn and twisted brass plate with the embossed words

START-O-MATIC
Electric Lighting Plant

Clearly it wasn't going to startomatically for me, but I happened to know that that didn't mean it was temperamental or fault prone, because above those words it was just possible to make out, in suitably decorative lettering, the immortal and venerated name of Lister, which, as anyone who ever heard the words 'generator' and 'she' used in the same context will understand, says it all. After its introduction in the 1940s. the Lister single-cylinder diesel became the standard in the industrial world for emergency power, indeed for all power in many isolated communities, and during four decades enjoyed an unrivalled reputation for economical running, reliability and ease of maintenance.

The prevalence nowadays of smaller, less over-engineered machines notwithstanding, the Lister's unique status, having begun as *indispensable*, has passed through *iconic* and arrived today at *cult*; and to cap it all it has a delightful sound, which is remarkable given that it generates – at least our one generates – so much of it. From time to time, when an easterly wind might have carried its distinctive *thump-thump-thump* in the direction of the McGarveys' houseboat on the other side of the sound, or our nearest neighbours on the mainland, we have apologised on the Lister's behalf. But nobody seems to mind. Having first been heard in an era towards the edge of living memory, it's as if by some quirk of accelerated evolution the engine note has become as background noise to our human senses; man-made but non-intrusive, like the sound of distant drums.

With some humility, therefore, I opened the control box and used a torch to examine the tangle of coloured wires, contacts and copper coils inside. I pursed my lips and drew air in through my teeth, made clicking noises with my tongue and shook my head like a professional. I even made skilful use of a screwdriver to probe around in there, without actually touching anything. Nothing worked: another try at the start button, another disheartening click, and I gave up. The generator, like the house, could wait. It was a useful tool, but hardly critical to our short-term survival. We could manage without fridge, electric lights, mobile phone chargers and (nobody said it was going to be easy) a television, at least until we managed to get an engineer out to the island.

Meanwhile, we enjoyed unhurried meals on the veranda, took the dogs for long walks along the foreshore and watched the sun go down from the top of Eagle Hill.

There is a spot up there beneath the craggy arms of an ancient mountain ash, high above the cabin, where the scattered remnants of a stone wall provide shelter as well as seating for a panoramic view of the entire length of the sound and much of the southern half of the lough. We would take a picnic up there and watch as a desultory late season procession of homeward-bound yachts passed by below,

rounding the southern point of Islandmore to enter the sound, turning briefly to windward to lower their sails and proceeding under power to their allotted moorings.

To the south lay the jewelled waters of the lough and beyond, the drumlined 'basket of eggs' countryside of Lecale in a hundred shades of green. In the far distance the impossibly two-dimensional purple cut-outs of Northern Ireland's highest peaks – Donard and Commedagh, Bearnagh and Binnian – rose clean-edged against the sky and added grandeur to beauty, defining and containing the whole: an exquisite arrangement of pearls and emeralds in a setting of deep amethyst.

On one excursion to the water's edge to throw sticks for the dogs, we opened our eyes to the well-stocked shellfish larder on our doorstep. We had always been aware that the mussels clinging in barnacle-encrusted colonies to the larger rocks just upshore from the low-water mark were there; but in the past we had ignored them, perhaps because we tended to arrive fully stocked for a short stay, with a dozen bulging supermarket bags in the bottom of the boat. In this new and necessarily post-consumer phase of our lives, though, we saw that kind of inverted self-sufficiency in a very different light – a don't-look-a-gift-horse-in-the-mouth light – and on only our second day on the island we headed out at low tide like a couple of kids and filled a half gallon bucket, not just with mussels but with cockles, which lie at random on the shingle, and by way of hors d'oeuvres, a brace of the oysters that account for Strangford Lough's place on the gastronomic map of Western Europe.

Back on the veranda we fetched a saucepan and filled a second bucket with seawater. Unlike Lynn, I wasn't raised in a fishing village, so I did as I was told: first removing the 'beard', a surprisingly strong fibrous mesh secreted from a gland within the mussel and used to gain a firm purchase on rocky surfaces, then scraping off the tiny barnacles with a penknife and lobbing the mussels in Lynn's direction for washing. Any already open were discarded, thrown over our shoulders into the three billion cubic metre recycling bin on the other side of the balustrade. The cockles, rounded and more mobile of habit than the mussels and having deep ridges on each of their perfectly symmetrical brindled halves, don't attract barnacles in the same way and were able to go straight into the pan ready for cooking.

There are as many possibilities for the flavouring and seasoning of steamed mussels as there are things to hand in the kitchen, and some of our visitors have shared with us little twists and subtleties of their own. Lynn tends to add white wine and finely chopped garlic to the water before steaming, and a squeeze of lemon or lime, some chopped coriander or perhaps chiles, maybe a dash of cream, after the shells have opened; but it's never the same twice.

I confess that the anticipated hors d'oeuvres didn't happen that day, only because I underestimated the stubbornness with which oysters are able to defend themselves. By the time I had hacked and hammered and pried with a blunt knife for ten minutes to try to get one open, with only a spoonful of blood – my own – to show for it, I was more than ready to concede. Magnanimous in defeat, I carried the pair of them with some ceremony to the end of the jetty and threw them back into the sea to fight another day.

I hope those particular oysters kept a low profile and make it to old age – apparently oysters can live for ten years or more – because within a few weeks we revisited the foreshore to try again, this time with reinforcements in the shape of young Sam Hawkins's father, John, who has had some experience of oysters. Once again we found a clutch of them very quickly. I wasn't about to admit my recent failure to John – I wouldn't give him the satisfaction – but I was careful to let him wield the knife and it turns out that with opening oyster shells, as with so many skills, there is a knack. Confidence is important too, and foreknowledge of the creature's strong instinct for self-preservation and how to circumvent it without losing fingers. (For the record: start at the hinge end of the shell and work the knife to left and right, not with a twisting action.) Even John had to work at it, but presently he sat back with a rather annoying smile on his face and a row of fine, plump oysters laid out in a tidy row on the bench beside him.

Just as I had deferred to John's superior skill in opening the oysters, Lynn deferred to his wife's in their preparation. Emma creamed some butter with garlic and finely chopped bacon; gave the oysters, still in their shells, a generous dollop each and popped them under the grill. A squeeze of lemon and that's it.

As Lynn always says, 'Dilencious.' We've had them that way ever since.

Eleven

Before leaving Scotland, we had put most of our belongings in storage and packed the van with what we imagined were the bare essentials for a year or two of living, if not out of suitcases, then at least away from – I was going to say 'home', but when we left Quilchena, home had ceased overnight to be somewhere we belonged and had become something aspirational instead. When a well-meaning yachting type later said to us 'So you're going to live on Islandmore. Where's home?' we realised with some embarrassment that we hadn't a clue. So let's just say that we had brought with us the absolute minimum for a year or two away from the normal accoutrements of life: power, heat, the shop around the corner, access right to the front door for something with wheels, ignition start, comfy seats – a roof. By the time we left for the island it was barely possible to pull down the roller door on the back of the van without hitting a length of six-by-two, the corner of a gas heater or a five-gallon jerry can of diesel.

With winter approaching, the critical things on our inventory had to do with staying warm in the cabin and dry on the water. Every fleece, woolly jumper, hat or scarf we possessed went into the back of the van. There would be all those crossings by boat in the coming months in every kind of weather, so we also invested in oilskins, sea boots with grip soles, and so-called waterproof gloves, naïvely believing there to be such a thing.

Then there were one or two what-if items, included at the behest of my family, who were touchingly concerned about our safety and wellbeing in a potentially hostile environment. Lynn's family in

Scotland, not having been to the island, were more relaxed about things, which was fine, since the last thing Lynn wanted to do was raise any fears, even if she harboured a few herself.

'What if,' my mother asked me, 'one of you goes in the water while you're crossing to the island at night? Or you are ashore or in Scotland and Lynn is on the island and she falls off the jetty?'

Not unreasonable worries, and all my mother had in mind were life jackets, and in the absence of a telephone link to the mainland, a second mobile phone. We could see that life jackets were a good idea, although I found out later from someone who knows these things that the fluorescent yellow one we found for Lynn, with its Presley-esque foam collar upstanding behind her head, really *is* a life jacket, whereas my more subtle grey collarless number is technically a buoyancy aid, the difference in no way being a technicality. Wearing either, apparently we could fall into the water any time we chose in the comforting knowledge that while we thrashed around wildly and reached for something more substantial to trust our lives to, like the side of the boat, we would at least stay alive as long as we stayed conscious. But if I should faint, have a heart attack or hit my head on something as I went over the side, that's a worry because whereas life jackets are designed to keep nose and mouth above the surface, the best a buoyancy aid can offer is something handy with which the emergency services can lift your admittedly floating, but possibly lifeless body out of the water later.

The other what-if involved a great deal of soul-searching. Lynn

does hate mobiles. Apart from the health risks, which worry both of us, it's the intrusion. She would be the first to say that her work as an artist depends to some extent on an insular, even a selfish, way of living. Her working method involves soaking up the landscape around her and expressing her emotional response to it in paint. The result is generally a semi-abstracted piece that relies on subtle interplays of colour, composition and tone to evoke, hopefully, a similar response in the viewer. It is an intuitive, intense and highly subjective process and often means long periods of introspection away from the studio, followed by frenetic bursts of creative activity within.

Despite the closeness of our relationship, therefore, Lynn's is paradoxically quite a solitary existence, and it couldn't be any other way. Neither of us being particularly gregarious, we have managed to find a happy equilibrium and I have learnt when to step back and certainly when to avoid the sixty-four-thousand dollar question: 'How's the work gone today?' When we were in Scotland, her studio was her refuge, her exclusion zone, and the very last thing she wanted in there was a telephone. Fortunately there was no land line to the studio and it was out of range of the cordless, but even when mobiles became ubiquitous, she held out against one on the reasonable grounds that if you have it, and friends and family know you have it, it seems rude to say that more often than not it's turned off.

Knowing her so well, I know she meant it when at first she simply said no to a mobile phone on the island. Sure, she might fall off the jetty, she might become ill, she might not know when I was coming home until I appeared, as it were, out of the shadowy gloom of a thick sea mist. But what did they do before mobiles? She would have the dogs, the wood-burning stove, her work, her own company; and crises could arise, and with as much finality, as easily on the mainland as on the island. The truth is, I think she succumbed to the phone as much to please me as her mother-in-law, and in the end we both agreed after only a few weeks that the poor unwanted little fellow had come into its own.

On my first return visit to Scotland, a fortnight after moving to the island, I arrived late on a dreich November evening and made up a camp bed on the floor of the workshop in Cowdenbeath. It would have been OK, even quite exciting, twenty years ago when I was starting in business and expected to sleep on workshop floors. But I wasn't twenty any more. I was tired, cold and, frankly, a little unhappy, and all I wanted was to be back with Lynn.

I was there to build a Colorado log bed for a customer in London and, as much as anything to keep occupied, I decided to make a start, selecting lengths of Douglas fir, milled in the round, and cutting them to size. I chopped out halving joints, two to a length, and assembled a log frame for the headboard using crisscross leather bindings and wooden pegs at the corners. The 'driftwood' finish requested by the customer, and arrived at years ago after many hours of experimentation and dozens of discarded timber off-cuts, involves a many-layered witch's brew of three parts this and two parts that and a final lightly buffed coat of the other; and even at this remove, with the original team from the Edinburgh business gone their separate ways, I would feel like a traitor if I put the recipe in print. While it cured, I cut a rectangle of soft-tanned Andalusian cow hide to size and punched slots around the edge with a chisel; laid it inside the log frame and stretched it gradually tight with thongs cut from the same hide, alternately working opposite sides in small increments to keep an even tension. It's the kind of work I usually enjoy. Every bed turns out subtly different and I can get quite absorbed by the process. It was well after midnight when I drove the last tack into the last strip of leather and stood the finished headboard against the table saw for a good look.

Had it not been for the pain in my back I would have worked all night and finished the whole bed, but I'd had enough and decided to turn in. I hobbled out into the darkness of the industrial estate, one of the many sprawling red-brick coal depots in Fife that were decommissioned with the closure of the mines in the eighties. It was raining hard and I half-ran across the old stack yard towards the toilet block. The place appeared deserted, so I nearly died when a bright light shone into my face and came bobbing in my direction from the narrow gap between two of the units. I held my arm in front of my eyes, peering feebly into the light.

A voice said: 'Working late?'

Normally that particular question makes me smile. It reminds me of when David and I, as teenagers, were driving fence posts into the ground beside the driveway of the big house at Seaforde. One of the police guard was passing on patrol and he stopped behind us and said, 'Hi.' We said 'Hi' back.

There was a long silence. Then he said: 'Doing a bit of fencing?'

I'm deeply ashamed, because I can't bear to see anyone embarrassed, to say that we both giggled.

On this occasion, though, I didn't even crack a smile.

I was still recovering from my fright when the voice behind the light said: 'Sorry about that. Just doing the rounds. I saw your light on. Jim Swanson.'

I didn't know the estate had a night watchman and I must admit I was pleased to see him. I offered him a cup of tea and we sat on a bench in the workshop under the orange glow of a gas heater and chatted. He eyed the camp bed in the corner more than once and it occurred to me that sleeping on the premises would probably be frowned on by the management; but he didn't say anything and I didn't raise it. He didn't fit the 'retired policeman' image of a security guard. He was small and grey and wore his uniform awkwardly, and while he was sitting, he tucked his cap behind him on the bench, out of sight – almost, I thought, by way of apology.

When he had gone, I turned off the heater and crawled into my sleeping bag. Rain was still hammering down onto the corrugated roof. The wind had got up and every so often, somewhere on the estate, the edge of a roof sheet was lifting and I heard a hollow rippling sound followed by a loud metallic *thwack*.

I felt too tired even to write my journal but I couldn't see much prospect of sleep. I thought about Lynn back on the island and dialled her mobile. She said she was reading by candlelight on the living-room window seat, with a dog on each side. The moon was full, so she had the curtains open, and she described the gleam coming off the surface of the jetty and the line of yachts lying at their moorings, head on to the current on the far side of Ringhaddy Sound: a little armada of ghost ships, their hulls in the moonlight glowing bone-white against a black sea.

It sounded, and indeed felt, I was pleased to discover, something like an image of home.

Twelve

The wind moved into the north sometime during our third week. Squally showers came whipping down the lough and the dogs hung around the front door of the cabin waiting to be let in. The feral flock of Canada geese massing in black and white on the fringes of the shallow bay opposite became noisy and restless, sensing the change of season and unsure what to do about it. Introduced as ornamentals by private collectors over three hundred years ago, they have almost, but not quite, lost their migratory impulse, and each autumn and spring, as their settled existence is comprehensively disrupted by the coming and going of enormous migrant flocks of pale-bellied brent geese on an annual passage from Europe to the Arctic and back, something seems to stir within them, and like a gathering of homesick expatriates who chatter feverishly about home and can't find their way to the airport, they jostle and bristle and honk themselves into a state of high agitation, martyrs to a vague and atrophied wanderlust – and stay put.

No wonder they get restless. Listening to them, I felt I understood their confusion, and Lynn, to be honest, will probably have shared it.

We retreated inside, where the cabin's limitations in the face of a cold wind became obvious. A fairly basic construction in the first place, eighty Irish winters and only irregular upkeep had taken their toll. Patchy, horizontal weatherboarding on the outside, an internal skin of vertical tongue and groove lining, whose tongues and grooves didn't always meet, and between the two a three-inch void without insulation meant that glimpses of the lough were by no means confined to the windows, and simply to use the corridor was to run a gauntlet of cold, and sometimes wet, blasts of sea air. Lynn conducted a quick survey, running her hand along the wall and laughing as she found more and more gaps. She kept saying, 'Feel this one! Oh no *way*! Put your hand here!' And finally, low down under one of the windows, she came upon the mother of all gaps, wide enough to permit a conversation with Rab, who had followed her progress down the cabin and was poking his nose through the wall from the outside.

'It's like living in a tent,' she said; and curiously enough she was echoing the feelings of an unfortunate German missionary, one Otto Schimming, who found himself stranded in the former German colony of Togoland, East Africa, when it was taken over by the British in 1916. He was shipped to England, then to the Isle of Man, as an enemy alien, and on entering an exactly similar hut at Knockaloe Internment Camp late that year, he wrote:

Thin, windy board barracks, no doubt suitable for the Tropics; against the wet, cold climate of the island they offer too little. It seems that the huts were intended for the Tropics ...

Late of East Africa, he adds ruefully, and with a touch of gallows humour: '... as, of course, were we prisoners'.

Schimming was one of 23,000 prisoners of war who passed through Knockaloe camp, and all of them lived and slept in sectional huts 30 feet long by 15 feet wide, which were generally butted together three in line and then paired ('A' huts and 'B' huts) to make one large hut 90 feet by 30 feet capable of taking 180 men.

The cabin on Islandmore, exactly 15 feet wide by 60 feet long without the little extensions at either end, represents two regular War Office pattern POW huts, and, who knows, maybe Schimming himself spent his war in it.

In fact, his descriptions of life in the enormous camp complex, with football, theatre, cinema and workshops (to generate revenue and prevent boredom, the camp produced anything from wicker baskets to Arts and Crafts cabinetry), are not especially bleak; but Schimming does come back again and again in his story to his two central themes: the barbed wire ('Everywhere the eye falls, *Stacheldraht, Stacheldraht, Stacheldraht*') and the climate. Unsurprisingly he contracted flu, and later pneumonia, in the camp; but while in hospital, he received the news he had been waiting for, that he was to be repatriated, and he

did make it home to write his account of camp life, published in 1919 as *Thirteen Months Behind Barbed Wire*. His final comment on the accommodation at Knockaloe is apropos: 'The windows of the "A" huts facing North, in never falls a sunbeam.'

All the huts were auctioned off in 1919, and it's probable that the Islandmore cabin is one of very few that have survived with more or less their original materials and layout: certainly none is thought to remain on the Isle of Man.

Fortunately, like the 'B' huts at Knockaloe, the cabin does get the sun for most of the day, facing just south of west; otherwise, as regards Schimming's 'thin, windy board barracks', not much has changed.

As a temporary measure, Lynn and I ran masking tape up and down the larger gaps, and Lynn made skilful use of her artist's acrylic to tone the resulting stripes with an umber wash, so that if we narrowed our eyes and took a relaxed view, the wall looked fine. Still, despite topping up the logs and turf in the living-room stove with coal, until the base of the flue pipe glowed red and alarming hissing sounds came from the back boiler, there was no way we were going to be able to rely on the stove to make an impact on the rest of the cabin. We tried opening the living-room door and allowing the heat to kind of roll along the corridor towards the bedroom, but it simply rolled under the front door, into the roof space and through the numerous smaller gaps we hadn't yet visited with masking tape. It certainly didn't do much for the kitchen and bedroom. So we closed the living-room door and laid a rolled up towel against the gap at the bottom, arranged the curtains to minimise the chinks between ourselves and the cold wall of glass above the window seat, and huddled in a super-heated, candlelit snug from which we mounted only essential expeditions to the coal bunker, the kitchen stove and the bathroom.

The thing is, it wasn't even that cold, at least by the standards of central Scotland at the same time of year or, as we found out later, Northern Ireland in December. But it *felt* cold, and not just because we were used to double glazing and radiators. The real reason hit home with some force when we turned in for the night. Not yet having re-supplied ourselves from the mainland, our oil lamps were still doing double duty and Lynn held the kitchen lamp in front of her to light the way to the bedroom. I was close behind and as she passed round the end of the bed something caught my eye for just a moment that made me double-take. I stared at the bed but whatever it was had disappeared and I wondered if I had imagined it.

'Bizarre,' I said. 'Go back a bit, can you?'

She took a backward step and there it was again. When the bed was directly in line with the lamp, the cover seemed to come to life, animated by a thousand points of reflected light. Droplets of condensation covered the whole surface and when I ran my hand across it, my fingers shone silver in the lamplight.

It may not have contributed much in terms of body warmth, but the heat from the stove must have been enough, in combination with the drop in temperature outside, to draw residual dampness from the carpets, from under the linoleum and probably from every absorbent surface in the cabin.

Bed, that night, didn't exactly beckon; but we had little choice other than to fold down the cover, turn the pillows damp side down and slip under the duvet. Neither of us managed much sleep and in the early hours Lynn took to blowing her nose, graduating to a dry and persistent half-cough. Giving up the fight, we lit a gas lamp and talked.

Lynn looked and sounded miserable but with a typically sweet sense of priorities, she said: 'What on earth are we going to do about the Hawkinses?'

Sam, and his little brother, Tom, and their parents would be our first guests on the island and were to arrive in two days, barely three weeks after our own arrival. They weren't expecting five-star accommodation, but colds and flu wouldn't be in their plans either.

'Hot-water bottles at night and electric blankets for an hour or two every day – and a blow heater,' was the best I could come up with.

'Powered by what?'

That was a good point. Without the generator, the little fish-shaped hot-water bottle Lynn had once put in my Christmas stocking might become our last line of defence against pneumonia. But a big red 'HAWKINS', in Sam's own hand, had been written across five pages of our diary since before we left Quilchena and the last thing we wanted was to uninvite them. We enjoyed their company but I hope they'll forgive me for saying that as our one-time nearest neighbours at Quilchena, they also represented an emotional link for us in time and place; a bridge, as it were, which we hadn't been forced to burn.

Besides, young Sam had begun packing his bag – bags – something over a month earlier. He was ready to roll, and as far as he was concerned that was all anybody needed to know.

So first thing in the morning I telephoned David to ask who looked after the generator, and how to get hold of them.

'That would be Dynamo Doherty,' he said.

Dynamo Doherty. Excellent.

'Can we arrange to get him out to the island as a matter of urgency?'

'Urgency? Certainly.' He hesitated. 'As long as he's still ...'

'Servicing Listers?'

'No, if he's still ...'

'What, alive?'

It was a joke, but poorly judged.

'No. He and I put the generator in twelve years ago and John was over seventy then. I'm just not sure if he might have retired.'

I left it to David, at his request, to phone Dynamo John Doherty and see what he said. I couldn't imagine, though, that the man would be into making the cold, wet and probably rough crossing to the island at his age, especially to wrestle with the Lister when he got there; and to my shame I actually began phoning round friends and contacts for the names of other diesel engineers while I waited. I feel guilty even saying that, because David phoned back to tell me that

John would be at Seaforde by ten o'clock the following day, and could I pick him up?

When I drove into David's yard next morning, John was standing waiting for me. I knew it was him by the steel tool box he carried in one hand and the rolled-up oilskins tucked under his arm. I certainly wouldn't have known by his age, and began to think that David might have been winding me up. Clearly his nickname had as much to do with his constitution as his area of expertise. I would have given this man sixty-five without being generous. Short and slightly bow-legged, he had a full head of silver hair and an astonishingly line-free face, which had the curious effect of making him seem younger the closer he came.

I jumped out of the car to shake his hand.

'You must be John. Thanks for coming so quick.'

He grinned. 'As the fellow says, you made it,' he said; and for some reason I pictured him speeding down the lane at first light in a cloud of dust, screeching to a stop and looking at his watch.

With that image fresh in my mind, I was quite relieved when he said: 'You drive. As the fellow says, you have a rough idea where you're going.'

I warmed to John immediately and on the way to the island I listened with rapt attention to his stories. He has known or worked with some of the great names of Northern Ireland engineering and motor sport, of which there have been many: in particular the self-taught genius Rex McCandless, clearly a personal hero of John's, whose many brainchildren included the Featherbed frame adopted by Norton Motorcycles for their racing machines; an all-terrain four-wheel-drive vehicle intended for the armed forces, which he called the Mule; and an industry-changing innovation in front suspension for which every motorcyclist since must have been grateful: telescopic forks.

My fascination for this kind of thing comes from stories told to me by my mother about her grandfather, William Sewell, who was a serious and versatile inventor himself. In the early 1900s, while he was based in Detroit, Michigan, he conceived and put into production the Sewell Cushion Wheel, which saw service with no fewer than two hundred city fire departments and dozens of truck fleets across the United States before being superseded by the first truly pneumatic tyre. We have an original Sewell factory catalogue from 1914, which proclaims the benefits of his innovative rubber-on-steel-on-wood design in the context of an exciting new age:

> The wonderful progress of the motor truck as a means of transportation has almost superseded any methods heretofore employed.

The wheel itself is on the cover, resplendently embossed in cross-sectional diagrammatic detail. Heavy wooden spokes radiate out from the hub to a steel rim, which carries in turn two layers of hardwood, of which the outermost is bonded to a final layer of rubber – the one that is in contact with the road. In these particulars the design is conventional enough, but my great-grandfather's refinement was a double set of flat rubber rings – somewhat like giant washers – which were riveted flat on to the wheel from both sides, sandwiching the three outer layers in such a way as to provide two shock-absorbing air gaps between the vehicle and the road: an innovation that will surely have made many a fireman, bouncing at speed along the cobbled streets of New York or Chicago, or the unpaved highways between, very happy.

The catalogue continues:

> The first set of Sewell Cushion Wheels, made in 1908, are still in operation on a Grabowsky truck owned by Marx Market, Detroit, and have run over seventy-five thousand miles, thus proving conclusively the sound principles of construction together with the lasting qualities of the Sewell Cushion Wheel.

At the boat park John pulled on his old green oilskins and strode off down the pontoons, entertaining me as he went. A good wind was blowing, but as it was still from the north, it was behind us for the crossing, and we stayed dry.

When I opened the door of the generator shed, John fell silent for a moment. He stood on the wooden step, his tool box held in front of him, and cocked his head to one side, smiling reassuringly at the Lister like a frontier sawbones called at the eleventh hour to minister to a needy and isolated patient. Gently he laid the box on the floor, dropped onto one knee and removed the cover of the control box with a screwdriver, which he placed within reach. He produced some kind of insulated probe, to which he attached an ordinary lamp-holder and light bulb by means of a crocodile clip and a short length of wire. A second wire, I think, ran from something else to something else and was affixed by a second crocodile clip. Holding the light bulb with one hand, John moved the probe around the various contacts and connectors, and every so often there would be a flash and the smell of burning, or the engine would turn over just once, or the bulb would momentarily glow; and John would murmur 'Yes. OK. Yes' under his breath, never flinching, never pausing. He removed wires and rerouted them, swapped them and stripped them and sometimes left them dangling in midair, as one by one he ticked the virtual check boxes of an enormous mental inventory of possibilities in his relentless and methodical search for the cause of the problem. At one point he left me lost for words by standing up long enough to say, 'I knew a Lister man who went out for years with nothing in his tool box but a hammer and a cold chisel'; and then went back to work.

He may have spent an hour at the job, it's hard to say. I was mesmerised, crouching with my back against the frame of the shed door and trying to learn something. Given, though, that John had travelled the long road from teenager to octogenarian in constant melioration of his art, the learning curve was bound to be steep and I forgive myself my abject and miserable failure.

Finally John straightened up for the second time and I prepared myself for another of his extremely short anecdotes, but this time his eyes were wide and bright and he was beaming hugely.

'As the fellow says, I think we're winning! Try the start button.'

Hardly able to contain myself, I did, and the shed was duly filled with the cacophonous – from close up anyway – sound of the Lister in full throat. We completely overreacted, slapping the workbench and punching the air as though we'd struck oil, and I went off to find Lynn so she too could enjoy our moment of triumph.

Celebrating with a cup of tea in the kitchen, John being teetotal, we heard more of his crack while the generator thudded away in the background, and I don't doubt that by the time John and I had stepped onto the With for the return journey, Lynn had put the Lister to work supplying power for three electric blankets and a blow heater in preparation for Sam's arrival next day.

I mean that literally: three electric blankets, a blow heater and some light bulbs is about the limit for the Lister, which gives just over four kilowatts of electricity. We always have to watch the overall load. We cannot, for example, run a washing machine on the island (a great disappointment for Lynn but also for Claire, who presented us with one as a house-warming gift); and if Lynn wants to use a hairdryer, she'd best make sure I'm not using the vacuum cleaner – it may be an unlikely scenario, but the combined load would be a very marginal three and a half kilowatts.

Motoring into the wind, John and I had a good soaking on the way to the pontoons. He faced backwards on the middle seat with his hood up over his head, but I do believe he would have been oblivious to the spray with or without his oilskins. He had to shout to be heard:

'I used to work with AJS motorcycles.'

'Oh yes?'

'Know what AJS stands for?'

'No,' I yelled.

'Aw Jesus Start.'

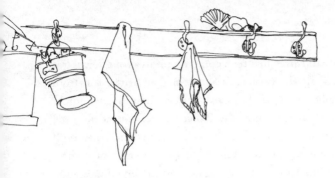

Thirteen

On the last day of November, the day after Dynamo Doherty's life-changing visit, I set off to collect Sam and his parents. It was a still, crisp and altogether invigorating day, one of several that would be rationed out in the coming week by a young and irresolute winter not yet into its stride: no need, certainly, to take extra weather gear in the boat for our guests. In any case, we knew from experience that John and Emma were Mr and Mrs Practical, and would come prepared. When their second child, Tom, was born, they were nearing the end of an elaborate barn conversion project that would shortly – if briefly – make them our nearest neighbours in Kinross-shire. They were all over the place, juggling joiners, removers, planners and buildings inspectors and tackling the site clearance work themselves; operating, it seemed, at the centre of a whirlwind whose course and culmination were fixed by the imminent transfer of their house in Edinburgh to new owners.

I'm sure Emma noticed when Tom popped into the world but to outside appearances he became part of the schedule, another entry on the Tasks side of the project completion chart, strapped in front of his mother while she attended to a roof over his head. His big brother, Sam, had meantime established for himself a floating role somewhere between Tasks and Resources, depending on his mood and presumably on commitments and distractions outwith his control.

On the morning of their arrival, to be on the safe side I threw in a pint-sized life jacket for Sam (there was nothing small enough for Tom, who would have to take his chances), which I found at the back of the generator shed. I intended to recommend it in strong terms but there was no need. At the boat park Sam emerged at the run from behind the car, fully kitted out and ready for anything the sea might throw at him. He shot past me in the direction of the peaceful little fleet of dinghies, in all shapes and sizes, which were tethered to both sides of the pontoon in listless resignation, like a string of quarter horses rope-tied to the fence between sessions in the branding corral. I said, 'Hey Sambamalambam, what about your life ja ...' before realising he had that covered too. He dead-stopped and turned to look at me, and I had to smile. He was 'Wee Hughie', off into the world for the first time, and as some of Elizabeth Shane's lines came into my mind, I couldn't help laughing:

> He cut the quarest figure,
> More stout nor thin,
> An' trotted right an' steady
> Wi' his toes turned in.

Only little bits of Sam were visible – some stray ginger hairs, his mother's blue eyes and the top half of a freckled white nose; the rest was buried beneath a truly arctic ensemble: fleecy cap with ear flaps; a full set of bright orange oilskins with a high collar, which, zipped all the way to the top, covered his lower face entirely; ski gloves, which might have been a size or two on the big side; and a happening pair of green and red Bob the Builder wellington boots. The outermost layer – the life jacket straining at its polypropylene straps and forcing Sam to hold his arms akimbo – was the final touch in his transformation into poor Wee Hughie; a latter-day, hi-tech nautical version of the early twentieth-century original, it's true, but with the same heroically, if barely disguised vulnerabilities, heading out there with a five-year-old's let-me-at-'em-but-don't-let-me-out-of-your-sight bravado.

In case Sam should imagine – perish the thought – that I was laughing *at* him, I said, 'Oops, sorry, didn't notice the life jacket; on you go'. And then, as he flew on towards the water, 'Stick to the MIDDLE of the pontoon; don't go too near the water!'

I glanced back at his parents, feeling a vague guilt that I hadn't stopped Sam and perhaps led him down there by the hand, but they were chatting and organising and getting themselves together, so either they trusted me not to introduce their son to the lough by drowning him in it or, more likely, they were relaxed enough to let him make his own mistakes and learn his own lessons – which makes, I have to say, perfect sense to me.

When we all got on board, Sam sat beside me on the stern seat. He frowned and twisted up his face and took a deep breath, an elaborate and anguished-looking build-up that used to make me think he was about to cry but which actually means he's working up to something important – an observation, a tricky question, a piece of man-to-man advice.

'Mike ...' he said.

'Yeah, Sam?'

'Can I drive?'

'The boat? I don't know. Are you qualified?'

'What?'

'How old are you?'

'Five. What does *qualified* mean?'

'It means you have to be old enough, and everybody has to call you Skipper.'

'How old?'

'Five.'

'Well can I drive then?'

'I suppose. Skip.'

'What?'

'Skip. From now on you're the skipper.'

'Cool!'

'Cool, *Capt'n*.'

'OK, Capt'n.'

I didn't hand over everything to Sam, because truthfully you have to be more than five, but I did give him the tiller arm and he 'steered' through the moorings while I kept a discreet contact on the throttle control and applied corrective pressure to the tiller now and then, like an obliging host at a Ouija board party, to ensure we motored in the general direction of the cabin. Sam was in his element, grinning and concentrating at the same time, perhaps tending ever so slightly towards overconfidence but pleased to have been made Head of Everything so early in his island adventure.

By contrast his father didn't look pleased at all; he pulled exactly the

same anguished face as Sam, except that John, I could swear, really was about to cry.

He said, 'I'm nearly ten times his age. I'm his father. Why can't I be skipper?'

Sam and I discussed briefly whether that was the kind of outburst that should really have consequences, like walking the plank or keelhauling, but we let it go. And anyway, Sam was becoming distracted by the reception party of three which had gathered on the jetty, waving, smiling, yapping and running round in circles.

'Lynn!'

'Woof!'

'Sam!'

'Woof woof!'

As we came in, the skipper abandoned the helm to the captain in cheerful, if arbitrary, recognition of our joint roles, and like a wing forward on a dash for touch, he scrambled towards the bow, handing off on anything that got in his way – his father's shoulder, the side of his mother's head – to give Lynn the kind of greeting you would expect at the end of six months rather than six weeks of separation. Of the slight shyness he had shown towards me earlier – not the parent-seeking, face-burying kind but Sam's own brand where he launches into a kind of distraction-babble and heads off in all directions with great purpose – there was no trace. They hugged as old pals and it struck me, not for the first time, that Lynn has an enviable knack of getting onto children's wavelengths without leaving the world of adults, which is why in her company they are never short of laughs, chat and the prospect of adventure shared.

On the veranda we toasted friends, fortune and (oh dear) good fishing. John is an avid fisherman and had asked tentatively if it was worth bringing a rod. I had vivid memories of long-ago expeditions with my father when the bottom of the boat was inches deep in mackerel (deep enough, in fact, to put my mother off mackerel for life: her memories are of hot summer evenings in the cabin kitchen frying waves of them for family and friends) and I had said yeah, sure, you bet – and we're the ones to catch them. It's true that Lynn and I hadn't fished on any of our recent island holidays but we had been looking forward to giving it a try with John and the others. With their arrival imminent, and in order to look as though I knew what I was doing, I asked John Scott about the best places to try for mackerel.

'Everyone has their own spots,' he said, 'but really, almost anywhere'; and I thought, Good, sounds promising. Then he added, 'Between July and September, that's when they're in the lough. Otherwise a bit of a waste of time.'

Not so good. Apparently cod could be had through the winter, but these very localised deep-feeding fish require special lures, a good knowledge of the best spots and how to place the boat directly over them and, most importantly, the kind of time and patience we were unlikely to have, given that it was a three-day visit, there would be six of us in the boat, aged from six months up, and it wasn't exactly high summer.

I didn't know how to tell John, so I decided not to. I hadn't reckoned, though, on his skill at reading people, an innate gift he has spent years honing in his professional life. (I am so not a corporate animal that until recently I thought they still had personnel departments, and when we first met John, and Lynn asked me about his line of work, I said he headed personnel, with a company called HR.) So even as we raised our glasses to the prospect of home-made Irish wheaten bread with mackerel pate, I could tell from the doubtful smile and the raised eyebrows that John suspected I was feeling less than confident; a suspicion no doubt confirmed during several lengthy and fruitless trolls of the lough in the following days, when I may have had trouble looking him in the eye.

In the end he managed to have the last word. Just to be sure I knew he knew, he wrote in our visitors' book:

Thanks for a perfectly adequate weekend.
We realise now that 'there are no fish in N Ireland.
... and that the mullet were all shot in the 70s.
We'll try to visit again if we're not washing
our hair.

Lots of love.

The Hawkins family
xx

I should explain about shooting the mullet. There is a shallow bay on the east side of the island where in calm weather during the summer months it's common around low tide to see the surface disturbed by the lazy twists and turns of a dozen mud-feeding grey mullet as they search for small invertebrates in as little as six inches of water. It's a languid, almost hypnotising performance, unless the fish are startled, when they churn the mud in a dash for deeper water and safety.

As a teenager, I tried every rod and line technique I knew to catch them – spinners, flies and even a worm and float – without success, and eventually hit on one answer by accident. As I wandered round the foreshore one afternoon, looking for old squeezy bottles, jam jars and bits of wood for target practice with a .22, I found myself at Sliddery Bay just as the retreating tide left behind a keyhole-shaped lagoon in the mud, midway across the bay. The mullet were in sportive form and it was so shallow that the occasional dorsal fin broke the surface as they cruised around one another in tight little loops and figure eights. Trying not to cast a shadow or make any sudden movements, I walked over the mud until it became too sticky for comfort. I picked out a fin, aimed the rifle at a point between that and the minuscule bow wave six or eight inches in front, and fired. There was just one half-hearted splash and a good-sized mullet turned belly-up, presenting its silvery underside to the sky. To retrieve it I had to fetch the dinghy, an operation in which I managed to generate so much hoopla and excitement back at the cabin that by the time I returned to the jetty later with my prize there was a suitably appreciative welcome committee of two policemen and the rest of the family.

I told John Hawkins this story when we got back from our third, ostensibly our last, fishing expedition, and on the basis of never say die we left the others at the cabin and motored round to Sliddery Bay in the fading light. Armed not with guns but with our skill and cunning as fishermen from way back, we spent a companionable half-hour at anchor in the quiet of the bay, cheerfully losing tackle in the seaweed, improvising weights with pebbles and generally thrashing the water until no living thing could possibly have been unaware of our presence.

John didn't feel the need to say much, which is an endearing thing and can mark, for me, the transition from acquaintance to friendship; and as we pulled up the anchor and slid over the black marble surface of Pawle Sound towards home there was something in his expression, a kind of worried wistfulness, that made me wonder if he was thinking about tomorrow, and the office, and all those human resources, and whether island life might not hold an unexpected and mildly unsettling appeal.

I may be wrong, he may have been thinking about the fabled mackerel of yesteryear.

Fourteen

The policemen who were waiting for me at the jetty the day I returned in triumph with my mullet came, as it were, in peace.

When he became prime minister in 1971, security around my father was greatly increased. Soldiers from the Ulster Defence Regiment augmented the police guard on the house at Seaforde and half a mile of barbed wire entanglement was stretched around the perimeter. The road escort was doubled to six men in two cars, and even when we crossed to Islandmore, the Royal Ulster Constabulary crossed with us.

A guard hut was brought over in sections and discretely erected among the trees a few yards from the cabin. It had a table with a bench and side chair; VHF radio; a Baby Belling gas cooker; and in the corner, a cylindrical paraffin heater whose low glow was the only light source during the hours of darkness and whose heat guaranteed a fumy fug day and night. Steps were cut into the bank between the hut and the foreshore, and stones cleared to form a path to left and right, which thirty years on is still visible as a faint depression. It led in a broadly rectangular circuit away from the guard hut and along the foreshore directly in front of the cabin, under the jetty, up the steep side of Eagle Hill, back behind the thorn hedge above the cabin, and down through the pine trees towards the water, returning to the hut via the foreshore from the opposite direction.

I think that, strictly speaking, the path was meant to be constantly patrolled. It was a time of escalating violence and every day brought new terrorist outrages somewhere in Northern Ireland. There were frequent death threats, shrugged off by my father until one Sunday morning he answered the telephone (on principle he never went ex-directory, believing it to be undemocratic and unfair to his constituents) and the caller told him not to take the family to church. That one, he did take half seriously – seriously enough to inform the police, who advised him not to go. He went anyway; he even took the family, and it was a most memorable service. There were marksmen in the surrounding fields and big men standing around the car park and at the church door, looking out of place. When we went in, they came in behind us and sat in the back row. After the service, the Reverend Cecil Adams, one of my father's oldest friends and the man who would later deliver his eulogy, shook hands with the congregation as they filed out. No one seemed particularly fazed; it was business as usual at Magherahamlet Presbyterian Church, which I suppose was a sign of the times.

Despite this background, depending on who happened to be on duty, the duration and regularity of patrols on Islandmore sometimes seemed to have little to do with the security climate and everything to do with the other kind. There was a bench at the highest point of the path, from which all approaches to the cabin could be observed, and on sunny afternoons a great deal of observation went on from up there. Some of the men took the job more seriously than others, but there was a sense that when rotas were drawn back at the station, island guard duty was far from being the short straw. It meant plain clothes, a relaxed routine and trips aboard *Horsa*, courtesy of Bob Scott, at each end of an eight-hour shift, with all the crack that that entailed.

Drawn for years from the same country police station, most of the guard had put in time at the house at Seaforde, so we knew them well enough; but the island offered opportunities for shared experiences, which meant that some of these men became good friends. Cecil McCann and I used to go fishing in a little rubber dinghy called *Pugs*, trolling endlessly up and down the sound without, now that I come to think of it, very much to show for it. Cecil was a man of few words with a dry, teasing sense of humour and a keen sense of responsibility. While we were on the water, he was careful to keep the cabin in sight, not because, as he liked to point out, fish hooks and inflatables don't go together, but because he was conscientious enough not to abandon his post entirely.

Several of the men, we almost lost. Tom Boyd, who shared David's interest in machinery and as a result spent much of his time on the island up to his elbows in engine oil, was on patrol in Newcastle, passing by a shoe shop, when a car pulled up beside him. A man stepped out and shot him at close range. The bullet hit Tom from the front and a little to the side, entering between his throat and his shoulder, exiting a hair's-breadth from his spine and passing on through the plate-glass window behind him, a box of shoes and the whole length of the shop, finally lodging in the back wall. He survived, returned to active duty and retired only a few years ago. On another occasion three or four of the men were travelling in the back of a police Land Rover when a single round came through the armoured bodywork and ricocheted to and fro between them. And when Raymond King, my best buddy from the guard, returned home after duty one night, he found a bomb on his doorstep. Most of us, I imagine, would have been inclined to leave it there and make ourselves scarce, but his family were inside, so he picked the thing up and carried it to an area of open ground in front of the house, where it exploded. Physically he was unharmed, but the mental scars have proved sufficiently deep to last a lifetime. I was fond of Raymond, and I think it was the aura of gentleness and quiet surrounding him that drew me to spend more time with him than with any of the others. He had – has – great generosity of spirit and, by example, he taught me an invaluable life lesson that I have always tried to observe: when it is said of someone that they don't suffer fools gladly, beware – there are few more unattractive character traits. Look to those who *do* suffer fools gladly.

Then there was big, round-faced Terry Edgar, who found something to smile at in most things and who felt relaxed enough one day to let me fire a round from his 9 mm. If that sounds a little indulgent, all I can say is that at the time it seemed the most natural thing in the world. Terry levered some wire off the face of a wooden gatepost and jammed in an empty cigarette packet. He took me back a few feet and stood behind me, reaching forward to put the gun in my right hand. He showed me how to grip my wrist with my left hand for extra support; patted and pulled and levered at my arms until they were more or less straight out in front of me; cocked the gun and thumbed the safety forward. I held it as steady as any thumping-hearted fourteen-year-old would-be cowboy would – steady enough, anyway, for Terry to decide the cabin, my foot, any passing boats and of course he himself were outside the line of fire – and concentrated hard on his final whispered instructions: 'Think about the target. Don't worry about the gun. Squeeze the trigger nice and smooth. Don't pull, squeeeeze. You can't miss.'

I squeezed, and missed so comprehensively that the very tip of the gatepost, a good foot above the target, disintegrated in a shower of white splinters, which came – I remember feeling surprised – in our direction, so that I ducked and spun around. Towards Terry, in fact, who moved fast for a big man, reaching to take the gun out of my hand. He dropped the magazine out of the butt, pulled back the slide and peered into the chamber to check that it was empty.

'Very good, Mike. Good.' He laughed. 'Not bad.'

My performance thus utterly, if tactfully, damned with faint praise, I felt I had somehow let him down, and ached to have another go. I blushed and stammered my thanks. He didn't offer me a second shot, which I totally understand, but funnily enough to this day I regard the whole thing as unfinished business. It's as if, somewhere, there's a 9 mm round with Gallaher's Special Filterless on it, and when I find it, I will become a man.

I had a lot of time for Constable John Kirkwood, perhaps because when it came to his job, he swam, by conviction as well as by disposition, resolutely against the flow, taking some stick from his colleagues as a result. Unlike one or two others, he took his duties extremely seriously. Earnest and shy, with a permanent questioning smile on his face and a tendency to hold his head a little down and to the side and to look up deferentially from under raised eyebrows when he spoke, he was and is one of nature's gentlemen. Always willing – perhaps needing – to help, John would appear when the boat required to be dragged into the water, or a box looked too heavy for my mother to carry down the jetty. He was even known to take a hammer on patrol and knock loose nails into the fence as he passed.

Once, in the house at Seaforde, my father's sleep was disturbed by a rhythmic clicking sound he couldn't quite place. He woke my mother and between them they pinned it down to somewhere outside the bedroom window in the direction of the stable yard. With typically scrupulous regard for police worries about his tendency to

present an easy target, Da opened the window and leaned out. There was a shadowy figure by the hedge which could only have been one of the guard: moonlight glinted off the peak of his cap and the barrel of a Sterling poked up behind his shoulders. As he turned he raised an arm in salute and dropped the other to his side. He was holding a pair of garden shears, and that was more than enough to identify him. My father, too, had a soft spot for John, and if he was upset by his wake-up call, he certainly didn't show it. It may have been four or five in the morning, but according to my mother, to judge by the casual conversation that followed, it could as easily have been teatime.

'All right, John.'

'Yes indeed, sir. Needed a bit of a clip.'

'Thanks very much, John. Nice night.'

'Hope I didn't wake you up, sir.'

John just had to be *doing*. It wasn't enough that, regardless of weather conditions, he left the guard hut to patrol the perimeter every thirty minutes through his shift, according to regulations. If the grass needed edging, he would take along a spade, and if the hedge was a little untidy, well …

Towards the end of 1977, a few months after my father was killed in a hunting accident, the guard at the house was first reduced and then quietly discontinued, and later the station from which the men were drawn was closed in a rationalisation exercise that marked the end for many of the smaller country police stations. The men, in time, were posted all over Northern Ireland and we lost touch with most of them. Then out of the blue my mother received a letter from John Kirkwood. He was well enough and living an hour and a half away. He said he was keen to visit and asked about everyone. In particular, he asked about Bobby Strain, the gardener whose entire working life, like his father's, had been spent in the garden at Seaforde and who for John was very much a kindred spirit – quiet, unassuming, straight. He seemed to have been prompted to write by news of his estranged brother's death in a London care home for people with a history of homelessness and alcohol abuse, and there was a sense of sadness and outreach in his letter.

My mother wrote back encouraging him to visit, and the upshot was that on a balmy afternoon in July I found myself wandering with John through the grounds at Seaforde, on the same peaceful and fragrant circuit he had tramped ad infinitum in uniform all those years before. Glimpsing *his* perspective, I discovered that in one way it wasn't so very different from my own. We had both left something behind here among the trees – for me a wonderful childhood, which had my father in it; and for John a period of robust and contributive purpose, which time and the vicissitudes of life seemed to have all but obliterated.

We passed under my favourite climbing tree, a venerable chestnut presumably planted when the house was built 170 years ago, whose lowest branch formed a deep crease where it emerged from the trunk. For a magical few months I would run into the woods every day when I got home from school and reach into that crease, standing on tiptoe and searching blindly with my fingers. Just occasionally I would be rewarded, and always with the same thing: a packet of chewy tobacco candy in a red and silver wrapper. I never found out who left it there and bizarrely enough I was too shy to ask, but when I took my treasure to the guard hut, more than one of the men used to give me knowing looks while I sat chewing in silence.

Anyway, if John knew the truth, he wasn't saying, and it looks as though my benefactor's identity will remain one of life's mysteries. After what seemed like years, the secret deposits of stringy candy one day simply stopped, and as children will, I accepted the loss without complaint or even comment, and after a while, stopped looking.

Directly in front of the house, where the trees become denser and quite dark, we stopped at the site of a night-time incident that had combined farce and high drama; even at this remove, the memory makes me laugh and shiver at the same time. It started when a dead tree came down in a winter storm. The crackle of dry branches splitting and breaking as they hit the ground sounded for all the world like automatic rifle fire, and of course pandemonium ensued. The army used to put flares among the trees, attached to trip wires, and no doubt in normal circumstances the men would have had a rough idea where they were. But roused from all points in the middle of the night and making their – presumably nervous – way through the undergrowth at a running crouch towards the source of the noise, whatever mental maps they had made for themselves in daylight seemed to let them down, and with the innocent-sounding *pop-pop* of half a dozen parachute flares, night turned briefly and embarrassingly into day. David, Claire and I watched the whole riveting spectacle from behind the curtains of our bedroom windows, high up on the gabled walls of the old house, as the men converged on the fallen tree, straightening up and making calm-down, patting movements in the air with their hands as they looked around, nodding and reassuring each other; exposed, foolish-looking, but at least alive.

John and I passed the old army hut, partially collapsed and barely noticeable among the trees due to the camouflage dusting of green mould that had spread across its walls, and emerged at the back of the house beside the police hut, even older but still sound and dry, the location, after the guard left, of head office for business ventures started by my brother and sister in turn. John looked for a long moment through the window, then turned and walked down the drive, away from the house, his hands clasped behind his back, silent and thoughtful. When he did speak, it was more to himself than to me, and if he seemed to belittle the tragedy of Northern Ireland during the worst of the Troubles, it was because he spoke not to the wider political issues but, like a soldier recalling his personal war, to the very private ones of advancing years and a badly missed sense of comradeship:

'The best years ever a man had,' he said. 'And they'll never come again.' A long pause. 'It depresses you.'

As we rounded the last bend in the drive, the white wooden gate came into view, and the road beyond. Just this side of the entrance there used to be a sentry box and a swinging triangular security barrier.

It had a steel plate with reflective diagonal stripes of orange and white. John must have stepped out of the box and swung that gate a thousand times. He stopped on the drive now and pointed into the distance, along the road to where it makes a turn and goes out of sight.

He said, 'I told the Inspector that day. They should never have been allowed closer than the turn.'

It was apropos of nothing, but I knew immediately what he was talking about. On Christmas Day in 1971, shortly after my father had made the appallingly difficult decision to reintroduce internment without trial for suspected terrorists, a group of republican protestors carrying a black coffin made their way in funereal silence down that road and gathered at the front gate. The police and UDR guard played the situation with professional restraint and remained passive but vigilant, awaiting developments. Someone made a short speech and when the demonstrators left in the same somewhat menacing silence in which they had arrived, they left the coffin behind them on the road. An inscription in white had been roughly painted on the lid and read:

BF ~ RIP

And it wasn't by any means my father's first seasonal greeting from the IRA that year. Over breakfast in the days leading up to Christmas, his mailbag had been unusually full, even for him, crammed with cards purportedly from internees within Long Kesh (later the Maze) prison. Many bore a cartoon sketch of my father with a swastika round his neck, and among the dozens of angry, obscene or threatening messages there was one that simply said:

Dear Brian
MERRY CHRISTMAS
Wish you were here.

break Fast.

Fifteen

Having assumed that we could plan our days the way we always had – on the basis of *what* we had to do, *when* we had to do it – we found that island life normally ran smoothly only when decisions on timing were predicated on the answer to one simple question: What about the state of the tide?

Early on, I learned that if we planned to leave the island at a given time the next day, it was worth knowing pretty accurately the previous evening where the tide would be. Each complete tidal cycle takes around twelve hours and forty-five minutes, depending on the age of the moon; so that in order, for example, to make sure the boat was accessible for an 8 a.m. start, it had to be tied to the jetty somewhere near the water's edge at around 7.30 p.m. the previous day. If I got it wrong by forty-five minutes either way, as I frequently did, I either had to wade down the jetty up to my knees and fish for the dinghy's bow rope with a boathook, or drag the stranded dinghy down the foreshore to the water. Neither operation was really a problem but both were a pain, and over the weeks I began to develop a subconscious tidal clock, self-advancing by thirty minutes a tide, so that if Lynn said, 'What about taking the boat round the back for fire wood tomorrow?' I would know, without stopping to work it out, that an hour before dark, say, the tide would be three-quarters in – useful when you're throwing bits of wood into the boat from the foreshore at the back of the island, or stacking them beside the cabin when you get back.

So by Christmas we were living to the rhythm of the tides. It

turned out to be especially important when gas canisters, bags of coal or drums of diesel had to be carried up the jetty: that is, every two or three days. Not only was the distance from the bottom of the jetty to the cabin a bit daunting at low tide; if the wind was blowing and the jetty hadn't been scrubbed for a week or two, the going was quite tricky. After rain and in darkness, it was very tricky indeed. Many times I managed to combine all these complications, and twice I paid the price with an unwanted swim. On one occasion, counting *one, two, three* to swing a half-hundredweight bag of anthracite from the centre thwart of the dinghy up onto the jetty, I forgot to let go on *three*; touched down ever so briefly on the slimy surface of the centre plank and carried on, along with the anthracite, all the way over the jetty and into the water. Reluctant to let go, I sank like a stone; but I managed to land on my feet and still had the bag in my arms when I staggered out of the water and across the foreshore to the coal bunker. On that particular night we really needed the heat.

It helped if the jetty was clean, so I took to scrubbing it once a week, following the incoming tide up the jetty with a long-handled deck scrubber during ten or twelve half-hourly visits, making use of the seawater to soften the accumulated slime and weed as I went. A strange thing happened during one of these operations, strange enough for people to look at me in a funny way when I tell them about it. I always finish by saying, 'Honestly!'

I had just scrubbed the latest stretch of jetty, and laid the brush down ahead of the advancing tide. Three-quarters of an hour later it was gone; I had left it too long. The rowing boat was tied near the far end of the jetty, well out of reach, so I said goodbye to the brush – I could even see the shaft sticking up out of the water as it floated north. A couple of hours went by. The tide turned. Another brush floated in from the north. People say it was the same brush, but it wasn't. It had a long wooden shaft like mine, but the head was made of wood, with natural bristles, whereas mine had been plastic, with synthetic green bristles. The sound was in a generous mood, that's all, and I said thank you and carried on scrubbing.

Like the state of the tide, but less variable, was the mere fact of the island's separation. There are other inhabited islands on Strangford Lough, but they tend to have causeway access, at least for a few hours per tide. In the absence of that very mixed blessing, and on the basis of 'If you can't beat 'em ...' we simply built the crossing into our routine. No use getting home to discover we'd forgotten milk: the nearest shop might be a five-minute run by road from the boat park, but it was the best part of an hour from jetty to jetty. Likewise, if we allowed the generator to get too low on diesel, it wasn't worth the trip: we simply shut it down and lived by candle – or oil – light. In any case, we tried not to run the generator for longer than necessary, not just because of the noise level but to avoid wear and tear – after years of operating for a few hours at a time, a few times a year, we were now expecting the old engine to do upwards of 150 hours a month. Our routine was to fire it up an hour or so after dark for the luxury of light, or television, at the press of a button, and to shut it down an hour before going to bed.

As the festive season approached we felt well enough organised to leave the island for a week or two without feeling that when we returned, we would be starting all over again: we had progressed, I suppose, from squatters, to campers, to residents in those first two months. I knew that Lynn had begun to see the place differently when she said, as I left one morning, 'When will you be home?' instead of 'When will you be back?' and that it would only be a matter of time before she brought herself, when we talked about the past, to say *Quilchena* rather than *Kinross*.

Our first Christmas was spent with my mother on the mainland, and we returned to Islandmore in the dying hours of the old year to prepare our customary welcome for the spirits of the new. Some years ago we borrowed an ancient and amiable tradition from the Pueblos of New Mexico, which involves lighting a fire at midnight as a guiding beacon for the benign spirits of the coming year. We have performed this simple ceremony ever since and of course this time it seemed to hold a special significance for us. By torchlight we made a circle of stones on the foreshore above high-water mark and laid in lengths of driftwood and some pine cones. The jetty became a bench table, on which we placed a bottle of champagne, chilled by the night air, two glasses, a bowl of blue corn chips and a warming dip of chipotle chile and Greek yoghurt. We lit the fire and the four of us sat hunched on the jetty like crows on a log, wreathed in pine-scented wood smoke, and waited for midnight. In the last thirty seconds we began a countdown, which prompted some furious and sustained off-the-beat accompaniment from the dogs, and on the notional stroke of twelve we popped the cork, clinked our glasses together and shared a few unspoken thoughts and prayers with the heavens, where a fiery upswirl of sparks made a dash to join the stars. Most expired almost immediately but one or two maintained an optimistic glow even as they flew over the treetops and out of sight.

Inside the immediate circle of the fire the heat was intense but in the darkness beyond, so was the cold. When the blaze finally began to weaken and we stood up to drag ourselves away, we caught our breath in the chill air. The grass crunched underfoot and on the handrail of the steps to the veranda a furry dressing of ice crystals gripped our gloves. At the top, slick decking boards and champagne conspired to take our feet from under us when we let go the rail to slip-slide gingerly in the direction of the front door, hand in hand, like novice skaters on a first uncertain exploration of the ice.

We put the dogs to bed near the stove in the living room and made our way along the corridor to the bedroom, breathing luminescent little halos onto the candles as we went. Desperate for warmth, we made the mistake, repeated since only in times of dire emergency, of lighting a portable gas fire beside the bed. We were happy enough to suffer the fumes as the price of heat, but we had no idea that so much moisture would be released into the atmosphere. Full on, it's more than four pints in eight hours, and it all has to go somewhere; so while we huddled in an imperfect and vaporous cocoon clutching hot-water bottles and weighed down by dressing gowns, fleecy blankets and an extra duvet, an insidious and uninvited guest joined us Trojan Horse-style in the bedroom, and prepared a nasty surprise for us while we slept. In the small hours Lynn got up to turn the gas off but the damage had already been done. When we prised ourselves out of bed in the morning, we found a layer of clear ice on the inside of the windows, our clothes hung limp and chill from hooks by the door, virtually unwearable, and there was even frost on the floorboards of the corridor. The atmosphere felt tremendously – pneumonially – unhealthy.

Outside, even the seaweed had acquired a silvery dusting of frost.

The water was very still and a pencil-thin column of smoke rose

from the saloon of the McGarveys' houseboat. Come midday we would be joined by my family for New Year's Day lunch, so following the McGarveys' example, I fetched the ash pan from the living-room stove, which still clung to life, and dumped the contents off the jetty; filled the firebox with coal and spun the draft control fully open. The fire picked up immediately but an intermittent and alarming *thunk-hiss-thunk* had started up in the corner cupboard, which houses the hot-water cylinder. Predictably, every time I opened the door to investigate the noise it stopped, but it was in the back of my mind that occasionally we used to let some hot water out of the system to prevent it boiling, so I went to the kitchen sink and turned on the hot tap. Nothing. I tried the cold, which is mains pressure, and got just one reluctant drip and a distant gurgling sound.

It didn't particularly worry or surprise me that the pipes had frozen, as the supply from the mainland is via a single alcathene pipe that runs below the sound and emerges along the foreshore to snake a rather erratic and sometimes exposed path through the trees to the cabin. But as I stood in the kitchen trying to come up with a sensible course of action, and thought back to my days in the flat renovation business in

Edinburgh when I did much of my own plumbing, the low *thunk* became a vibration punctuated by louder *clanks* and then a continuous metallic rattling that I could actually feel through my feet, and I began to have visions of the copper cylinder popping its fixings and crashing through the roof on a mushrooming cloud of super-heated steam.

Calling for Lynn to come and help, I trotted back to the living room and shut the draft on the stove down fully, which helped to the extent that the roiling, bubbling sound coming from the back boiler inside subsided a little. But the one-man band in the cylinder cupboard was still banging it out and in desperation I attempted something which for sheer futility beat even the disjointed, half-remembered and in fact useless bits of information on gravity feed and thermal vacuum that were racing around my brain.

I struggled with the stirrings of panic and managed, I thought, to *appear* reasonably calm, but as always in crisis moments my words refused to match my demeanour. When Lynn appeared I asked her to please stay in the living room and listen for the tap, but what actually came out, confusingly, was 'Pea stain the ling room and list four taps.'

She said, 'What?' and fixed me with a calm-down-let's-try-again look, with which I am quite familiar.

So I said it again, slowly. Then I tipped out the contents of one of the kitchen drawers, grabbed the rather smart designer blow torch Lynn uses to finish her amazing *crème brûlées*, and sprinted outside and round to the back of the house, where I was confronted with enough black alcathene pipe to keep a whole squad of plumbers with blow torches – real ones, made for more than caramelising sugar – busy. The pipe emerged from the bank, looped a few feet in the air, disappeared under the cabin, popped out through one of the bedroom walls and dove back into the bank again, heading in a series of Nessie-like undulations in the direction of the northeast corner of the cabin; behind which, I knew, lurked our increasingly boisterous hot-water cylinder.

Lacking a better plan, I set to and played the tiny flame slowly to and fro over the pipe, starting at the corner of the cabin and working back towards the bank. Every so often I looked hopefully over at Lynn, who was standing behind the living-room window, for a signal that we had a flow of water, but each time she shook her head and pointed towards the corner cupboard with a look which at the time

I took to be exasperation, but which turned out later to have been real fear.

I felt there was at least an element of logic, however desperate, in my efforts, since near the top of the bank above me, about sixty feet away – not so very far – I could see the cold-water storage tank perched on its grassy ledge, and unless it contained nothing but solid ice right to the bottom, there had to be water at the outflow, and I reasoned that the frozen pipe must be somewhere between the tank and the cabin. So I continued doggedly uphill, pausing at the numerous points where the pipe wasn't covered by an insulating layer of earth, or at least grass, and concentrating my efforts there.

Inevitably, though, I was running out of ammunition. The mighty flame-thrower became a Bunsen burner and finally a cigarette lighter, at whose feeble flame even sugar would have laughed. Defeated, I stood up and looked again in Lynn's direction; but I couldn't see her through the window and assumed, at first, that the inside of the glass was simply steamed up. Then the window flew open and slammed back against the side of the cabin, a milky grey cloud billowed out through the opening, and Lynn reappeared at its centre, or at least her arms reappeared, making frantic 'Stop! Enough! Shut it off!!' scissor movements in the air, as if there was something I *could* shut off. Instead, I scrambled down the bank at speed; fell over, got up again and ran round into the cabin.

The living room was greatly changed. The open door was barricaded from the inside by a jumbled heap of furniture. I lifted a coffee table off the top and climbed over a sofa to get in. Lynn was standing by the corner cupboard in half an inch of gently steaming water, hands on hips, breathing heavily and looking distinctly shell-shocked. Though she had clearly acted pre-emptively, and fast, to clear the room of furniture, rugs – everything, in fact, that wasn't, like the carpet, nailed down – she had been too late to save the television, the stereo or the vacuum cleaner, all of which had lived in the hot cupboard directly under the tank, and all of which must have suffered the full impact of the first blast of steam and water. The old ten-inch black-and-white Grundig TV, exposed in the seventies to too many episodes of *Kojak*, of which my father was a fan, had assumed a melodramatic moment-of-death pose, tilted backwards on a stool in the middle of the floor and bleeding water from every orifice, its big square eye staring sightlessly at the ceiling. From somewhere near the back wall I could hear the sound of running water as the contents of the tank escaped through the floorboards. Thank goodness, I remember thinking, we don't have neighbours to worry about.

I squelched over to examine the tank. The inlet pipe at the base, the same one I had struggled with on the other side of the wall, had popped clean out, brass fittings and all; the victim, I supposed, of the clash of irresistible force (a head of steam) and immovable object (the elusive ice somewhere along its length). The last of the hot water was still glugging out through the resulting hole, and the end of the supply pipe dangled ominously in midair to the side, a kind of watery Sword of Damocles that needed only the encouragement of a slight thaw – a process I had helpfully got under way already – before another fifty gallons of water would be decanted onto the living-room floor from the cold tank outside.

I managed a temporary repair by working the pipe back out through the cabin wall, kinking it and tying it back on itself with a length of twine. Lynn and I then had a short discussion about whether or not to leave the stove burning, our worry being that the remaining water in the little back boiler, still bubbling quietly, would presumably boil away altogether eventually for lack of a supply, and for no particular reason we felt that that might be a bad thing.

We tried a few plumbers and got only answering machines and then it dawned on us that not only was it New Year's Day, we were also in the grip of the first real freeze-up of winter, when emergency plumbers would be awash, so to speak, with emergencies. Meantime, while we stood and swithered, a through draught from the front door to the back window, given extra bite by the natural accelerant of the intervening corridor, had reduced the inside temperature to something close to the outside, which of course was something below freezing. We decided to give up on finding a plumber able to make the boat trip at short notice, and erring on the side of caution, we shovelled all the hot coals from the stove into steel buckets and carried them outside in choking relays.

When we were done, we stood and looked at each other, and Lynn said reasonably: 'We must be off our rockers.'

She looked at her watch.

'Everyone arrives in an hour. There's nothing cooked. The living room is a bomb site. There's no vacuum, no water, no stove and it … is … SOO … COLD!'

'There's always the generator,' I said.

I was thinking of the blow heater, and secretly wished I had thought earlier of the hairdryer as a possible alternative to the chef's blow torch.

I went round the side to the generator shed, and fortunately before going in I checked the water in the 45-gallon drum outside. The drum, which stands on a platform against the back wall and has inch-and-a-quarter IN and OUT pipes at the top and bottom respectively, supplies coolant to the Lister's engine by a simple gravity feed. If the feed is interrupted, I don't know what happens, but I know it's not good. There were a couple of inches of ice on the surface of the water, but worse, the plastic pipes had frozen solid. I didn't dare try to start the engine, and returned to Lynn as the bearer of bad news.

'Forget the generator,' I said. 'Sorry.'

We both laughed – a nervous, shivery, blow-on-your-hands-and-rub-them-together laugh – and agreed there was nothing for it but to wheel out the gas heater for the second time in twelve hours, and to trust to the power of a weak January sun, just then peeping over the crest of Eagle Hill, to restore a flow of water to the kitchen sink and, equally importantly – certainly from our visitors' point of view – to the bathroom.

In the end it all came together, after a fashion. With not a cloud in the sky, by the time my mother called from the boat park to say she had arrived, the sun had managed to take care of the water supply, the outside temperature and even, by degrees, the cabin itself. Nine of us sat down in surprising comfort to a late lunch at the kitchen table, sandwiched between the gas heater – shamelessly rehabilitated as an old friend – and the Newhome Everclean Cabaret Four De Luxe gas cooker, the last word in 1970, whose four rings, eye-level grill and convenient, capacious and of course everclean oven were all turned up to the max and made a noise in the background like a small jet engine. With no incentive, for obvious reasons, to move to the living room after eating, we took our time over the meal: parsnip soup, turkey in chestnut sauce with sweet potato mash, and the last of Lynn's mince pies from Christmas.

I love my family dearly and it felt good to have everyone together, and in our own space – something that had been next to impossible, with all our disparate commitments and the constraints of travel, back in Scotland. I looked around the table, happy that in the coming months we could do this more often, and in particular I looked at my mother and thought: Every cloud …

As a bonus, my sister even found us a plumber. Claire could thoroughly recommend Andy, she said. He had done all kinds of plumbing and electrical work for her over the years. He was obliging and he knew what he was doing. She phoned him up there and then and arranged for him to come to the boat park next morning. This was quite a coup, as he was apparently greatly in demand, but just how much of a coup it really was she had no way of knowing, because, as it turned out, Andy was one of the (presumably) very few aquaphobic plumbers in the area. Not the contradiction in terms it might seem, his difficulty seemed to be not with the kind of water that flows through pipes in a predictable way but the kind that deranged people venture onto in boats; the kind that is deep and dark and anything but predictable.

Forewarned, we would have paid more attention to the digital weather forecaster Claire had given us for Christmas, which showed the barometric pressure to be falling, and on a steepening curve, as the evening became greyer and the surface of the sound, so recently a serene and limpid turquoise, turned fractious and bleakly opaque.

That evening, having ferried everyone to the boat park, I returned on something more than a gentle swell but nevertheless thought only genial and optimistic thoughts about tomorrow, about hot running water and all the comforts of home.

the diver

Sixteen

At no single point in the With is it possible to be more than a couple of feet from the water. Unsurprisingly in a small boat, there is no handrail, nothing to lean against or hold on to, and no canvas cuddy in the bow under which protection might be sought from real or imagined perils.

What there is, apart from a fixed wooden locker strong enough to support the helmsman in the stern, is a pair of side-to-side thwarts, or bench seats, one near the bow and another more or less amidships, between which a third runs fore and aft down the centre-line of the boat to make up the bar, as it were, of a capital H. It's not something I had thought about before, but if you sit on the aft seat facing to the front, it is possible to plant a leg on either side of the middle seat and grip it tightly between your knees; in this way achieving a limpet-like adhesion to the boat, which no amount of pitching, slamming or corkscrewing can compromise.

Andy the aquaphobic plumber adopted this unconventional and rather formal-looking position – ramrod straight, eyes to the front, his canvas tool bag hugged close to his chest – while we were still tied up to the pontoons. Before getting into the boat myself, I saw him side on, from which angle he resembled the top-hatted groom on the jockey seat of an undertaker's brougham, grim-faced and rigid. The boat coggled a little when I stepped aboard, but he didn't lean in the opposite direction to compensate, or put his hand on the gunwale; he remained perpendicular to the boat, just another fixture, and they dipped and rocked together in perfect concert.

I sat behind him on the stern seat and leaned forward to ask if he was OK.

'Yes,' he said unconvincingly, staring straight ahead, and I pushed off and turned the boat into what by that time was not far short of a gale.

A wind of gale strength is given as Force Eight on the Beaufort Scale, with a speed of 39 to 46 miles per hour; above that, in incremental steps of 6 or 8 miles per hour, come Severe Gale, Storm, Violent Storm; and at over 72 per miles per hour, Hurricane or Force Twelve. To give some idea of scale: the storm of October 1989 that caused so much devastation throughout the British Isles was just that – a storm.

Only once in the last twenty-five years has Ringhaddy been visited by hurricane force winds, and on that occasion, in February 1982, my Uncle Dennis watched from his house on the mainland as a dinghy was torn from the pontoons and sent like a skimming stone across the sound, cartwheeling over the fields and hedges of Islandmore and disappearing behind the ridge on Eagle Hill.

Late that afternoon, at the height of the wind, he took a remarkable photograph from the north end of the sound, looking diagonally across towards the cabin: the sun has just broken the lower edge of a curtain of dirty grey cloud, flooding gold into a strip of clear sky underneath and punching out the crowns of the Scots pines by the cabin. Beyond Islandmore, the outline of Ringdufferin Point, which defines the boundary of sea and sky, appears as a faint and liquescent brushstroke of burnt umber through a veil of horizontal spray. The sound itself, with its top dressing of silvery plumes layered over streaks of sepia where the sun has penetrated an extra cargo of weed and silty foam, has the rich translucence, the good-enough-to-eat quality, of a freshly pulled glass of Irish stout, backlit by candles. A dozen yachts face dead into the wind, trailing tattered banners of muslin spray from their rigging, hanging at crazy angles to the sea and blasted back against their mooring chains until some of the buoys have lifted clear of the water. On Islandmore the cabin is just discernible, its drenched and gleaming front wall picked out by the sun: an insignificant, transitory-looking structure – unfairly placed, you would think, in the path of such careless elemental forces.

In an anchorage with as much natural shelter as Ringhaddy, the way in which extreme conditions are experienced depends as much on the wind's direction as its speed; and at anything more than, say, twenty-five miles an hour, a southwesterly wind, funnelling up the length of the sound and hitting the front of the cabin a glancing blow as it goes, will affect the surface of the water in a more or less dramatic way according to how it interacts with the third crucial determiner – the current state of the tide. On the flood, that's to say when the lough is receiving water from the open sea to the south and the direction of flow is from south to north, wind and tide advance, as it were, in harmony, albeit at different speeds, and the wave pattern tends to be long and low, with an even scattering of parallel white riffs, where the wind, like a scythe in a wheat field, has sliced the tops off any waves raising their heads above the rest. The overall effect is of a swift but fairly predictable progress of sea, and head on in a small boat a soaking is more likely than a scare.

On the ebb, however, when the run of water is north to south and wind and tide are in opposition, the effect is as of a pair of sumo wrestlers meeting on the mat: with a great deal of energy to be released and only the dense and relatively unyielding water below, most of the explosive force is directed upwards into the air and the result is a short, steep-sided, choppy sea, where high, and highly unpredictable, white caps crowd each other in fast and chaotic profusion. A small boat head on to the wind can find itself perched one moment atop a foamy knife edge and dropped the next into an abyss, at whose floor the bow can pierce the water and scoop a barrelful of sea onto the wrong side of the hull. With each ascent more ponderous than the last, before long there is the risk of being (to use a technical and succinctly accurate term) swamped. With two on board, the first recourse is for the crew to bale out as much water in as little time as possible to try to retain buoyancy, and for the helmsman to keep the boat head on to the wind and work the throttle control in such a way as to ride, rather than break the waves.

Without a crew, or when the movement of the boat makes it physically difficult to put any real effect into baling, there may come a point when the sea cannot be ridden in this way and buoyancy is compromised by the extra payload of water; and in that event the simple-sounding but often heart-stopping manoeuvre of turning around and going with, or across, the wind is the next option, however unattractive.

Thank goodness Andy was in perfect – I cannot say, blissful – ignorance of all this, because as luck would have it, conditions were really quite poor. It would be wrong to say that the seas were mountainous, the Sirens were calling from the rocks, or even that the little ship couldn't have taken this kind of abuse much longer; but a swiftly ebbing tide was running head on into a strong southwesterly wind, and as crossings of Ringhaddy Sound go, it was alarming enough.

I found myself wishing with religious fervour I had brought along a life jacket for Andy, and I had an unconvincing stab at shouting reassurances to him over the wind that everything was fine, that we would be there in five minutes; but I don't think he understood because when he replied he managed the unlikely feat of yelling plaintively: 'How long does it take?'

I leaned forward and said into his ear: 'Five minutes!'

In return I expected 'OK then' or 'Is there a short cut?', or even 'Is it too late to turn back?', but I think in some strange way Andy had left the boat and was drifting away, clinging to a private catatonic life raft of his own devising and shutting out, as best he could, the nightmare of his situation.

Had I not been so close to him I probably wouldn't have caught his reply. In a dull and insulated monotone he said again: 'How long does it take?'

Poor Andy. It was probably the longest ten minutes of his life. Were it not for his family on the mainland, he might have stayed on Islandmore indefinitely, living rough in the derelict farmhouse further north and surviving on shore mussels and sheep's milk.

As it was, on the plumbing front he lived entirely up to his reputation. By the end of the day he had restored water to the hot tank and we were able to relight the stove. By a nice sense of timing the tide had turned and the wind had moderated significantly and gone round to the south, behind Eagle Hill; so our return journey to the pontoons was comfortable and almost dry. Andy seemed fairly relaxed and I even began to wonder if he had conquered some fears.

He had made a point of telling us that to prevent the pipe parting company with the cylinder in the future, the last few feet of alcathene should be replaced by copper as soon as possible, and I asked him rather diffidently if he would come back in a little while to do the job.

'Give me a call,' he said. 'Give me a call.'

I thanked him and said sorry about the weather, an oblique apology if ever there was one, and over the next few days we periodically felt around the junction of the pipe with the tank for signs of water. Sure enough, what started as the very slightest suggestion of moisture developed over a week into a full-blown drip, and we took to putting a mug underneath. I left a message on Andy's answering machine: I was sorry to come back to him so soon, but would he mind returning to fit the copper pipe?

As the mug was replaced by a saucepan, then a big plastic mixing bowl and finally a bucket, my messages to Andy became increasingly desperate, until I more or less begged him to come back to the island. That he never did return my calls tells me not that he is unhelpful but that island life in wintertime is not for everyone.

Even Lynn, who doesn't scare easily, wobbled a little during a late winter expedition to Portaferry, six miles to the south, for lunch at The Narrows restaurant. We had with us Allan MacDonald, a black-haired, blue-eyed Highlander who studied painting with Lynn at Edinburgh College of Art. Allan is the kind of artist who ropes himself to clifftops for extra realism. He works in oils on large canvasses and his landscapes – crags and trees, crashing waves and big skies – have an epic quality that makes you stand and stare. He doesn't like the comparison, because it's fluky and admittedly somewhat facile, but from my strictly lay perspective, his work is reminiscent of Tom Thomson and the Group of Seven Canadian impressionists who took their canoes and tents to the remote lakes and forests of northern Ontario during the 1920s, camping there for months at a time; and, of course, anything that's vaguely North American, especially wilderness North American, has my instant approval.

I was in two minds whether to make the trip to Portaferry because a strengthening southerly breeze promised a certain amount of splashing over the starboard bow as we motored southeast across the centre of the lough. However, at that time you were guaranteed a gastronomic reward by The Narrows' lunchtime menu and having prepared ourselves with a very light breakfast, we were keen to go.

I told Allan the crossing would be a bit lumpy and asked if he was OK with boats – something I tend to take for granted with guests and plumbers alike, which is unfair.

He smiled and said cheerfully, 'I wouldn't know one way or the other.' Then he added: 'You're the boss.'

I hadn't thought of myself as the boss, but that is not a good attitude because, as the next few hours would show, it's vital that at least one person takes responsibility for the safety of all and keeps an overview of things – stands ready, as one of our yachting guru friends, Steve 'Early and Decisive Action' McColl, would say, to take early and decisive action.

Seventeen

My favourite lecturer at Aberdeen university, who took us for delict and contract, used to say that in order to immunise himself against a later charge that he had failed to have a document properly, that's to say, legally, signed by a client, a solicitor should always be able to say under oath, 'It is my *invariable practice* to require the attendance of two qualified witnesses, etc., etc.' even when − especially when − he cannot recall the actual occasion of the signing.

I have Dr Blaikie to thank, therefore, that when my Uncle Dennis, who has vast experience of the sea and who watches over us with a ... well, with an avuncular eye, asked me some weeks after our Portaferry adventure whether I had been ready for all eventualities on that February morning and, in particular, whether we had been wearing life jackets, I was able to say that it is my *invariable practice* to carry not just life jackets but extra fuel, an anchor (in case of engine failure), a pair of oars, binoculars, a torch and the Admiralty chart of Strangford Lough when we venture outside Ringhaddy Sound. 'I didn't ask if you had life jackets, I asked if you were wearing them,' he said, and although there was a twinkle in his eye, I found myself thirty-five years younger and standing in the headmaster's office, mumbling and stuttering and changing the subject. Leaving that aside, however, I reckon that we were pretty well equipped.

The first part of the trip was delightful. There was a good breeze but it was bright, and surprisingly warm. The tide was high, so we were able to get plenty of shelter by passing inside the Black Rock and close to Ringdufferin Point, an area where massive boulders, covered with barnacles and lacking the natural cushion of weed that can take the sting out of a collision, lie treacherously close to the surface at anything below half-tide.

I was keen to show Allan the stand of pines at Ringdufferin, which has one of the busiest heronries in the area, and we drifted very close to shore to get a good look with binoculars. To exaggerate only a little, there were herons everywhere. With the mating season round the corner, they were quite animated, moving freely among the trees, flap-jumping from crown to crown and making harsh and croaky *kah-rahk kah-rahk* calls with competitive enthusiasm. It was such a contrast to the inscrutable stillness with which they fish in the shallows.

Lynn said, 'I wonder which one is ours?'

'You mean Mr Heron?'

This was the imaginative name we had given to a solitary bird which almost every morning since before Christmas had come to the same spot beneath the jetty at first light. He would stand poised and motionless, his head cocked to one side and his neck held in a deceptively relaxed-looking S shape, waiting for some hapless sprat to swim within striking distance. Then the neck would slowly uncoil and stretch forwards and downwards at a shallow angle to the water, and the legs would inch forward, each foot clearing the surface with every step and disappearing again without a ripple. The strike itself was something to see, his closed beak operating as something between a dagger and a steam hammer, spearing the fish several times before snatching it clear of the water and juggling it into position so that it could be dropped headfirst down the not-so-little red lane of his prodigiously long and ruler-straight gullet.

For a while we were in the habit of saying to our visitors, 'You've got to see the heron. Amazing to watch!' And we would set up breakfast in the bay window and wait for him to appear. And wait, and wait … It's the oddest thing but he seemed to know when there were strangers on the island and the morning performance never did happen as billed. Once or twice he glided in but moments after touchdown he was in the air again, lumbering off in no particular hurry to try some other, perhaps less touristy spot for his fishing.

'Believe me,' I once said to John Hawkins, 'as soon as you guys leave he'll be back'; to which John replied quietly, 'Of course he will, Mike. Of course he will.'

Anyway, by the time we emerged from the lee of Dunnyneil – a small island at more or less the halfway point to Portaferry, somewhat snail-shaped, comprising a pair of unequal mounds separated by a shingle isthmus which is normally covered at high tide – the wind had increased to perhaps twenty-five knots, the tide had begun to ebb and we were confronted dead ahead with a bar of angry-looking white water of indeterminate width. It was still a good way off but even at a distance it had a nasty look about it. I thought we might be able to go around, so I throttled back and stood up on the stern locker to have a better look.

These days it would be a simple decision to make: there being no point whatsoever in motoring willingly into trouble, I would turn back and head for home. But ignorance is bliss. I couldn't see a way round the swath of broken water ahead but it seemed to be only a few hundred yards across, and beyond it conditions looked invitingly quiet. I didn't know that this is the area where after half an hour of slack water on either side of high tide, the lough begins, with or without an adverse wind, to bunch and whirl like bath water when the plug is pulled, crowding the natural bottleneck of the Narrows before rushing through towards the Irish Sea. Nor did I know that I might have been able to avoid it altogether by moving far enough to the west, beyond the tidal run – I found that out from my uncle later. So in blind faith I handed out the life jackets, warned Lynn and Allan to face the stern, pull up their hoods and get ready for a soaking, and held a course for Portaferry.

The hull of the With is made up of a sealed sandwich of fibreglass containing high density foam, and the manufacturers claim she is unsinkable. That's not to say that if she fills up with water, she won't disappear, only that, all things being equal, she should retain neutral buoyancy, 'floating' just below the surface and not actually going to the bottom. The trouble is that all things are not necessarily equal, and the effect of a heavy outboard motor and two or three panicky occupants is hard to predict and even harder to test. Still, that was the comforting thought that came into my mind as the With began to plunge, throwing up twin cascades of water from under the bow, which were taken by the wind and redistributed over the three of us: *the manufacturers do claim that she is unsinkable.*

'The manufacturers claim she is unsinkable!' I shouted happily.

Lynn and Allan raised their hooded heads and gave me looks that discouraged further attempts at levity.

I glanced back towards Dunnyneil. The lee side of the larger, tree-covered mound would offer a sheltered bolt hole if we needed it later, but the little island was nearly a mile behind us now and I was a bit alarmed to see that we were already in such a deep swell that every few seconds it disappeared entirely, lost below the line of an ever-changing and uncomfortably near horizon.

The only way I could keep an eye on our direction and judge the state of the water immediately in front of us was to crouch on top of the stern locker, gripping the tiller arm with one hand and the side of the boat with the other. The full force of the spray was hitting my face and I narrowed my eyes and yanked at the peak of my oilskin hood. I couldn't keep water out of my mouth and nose and for some reason my frequent splutters were starting to make me laugh. In this respect I was conspicuously alone: Lynn's dark eyes drilled into me from under a dark frown and only her eyebrows moved as her expression flickered from accusing, to questioning, to a mute and determinedly private concern.

One especially steep wave hoisted us so high that the bow pointed skywards, then dumped us with a bone-shaking crash into the belly of the next wave; opening, at the same time, a hairline crack in Lynn's composure.

Her voice rising, she said, 'I don't like this, Mike. I don't like this!'

And when I saw how frightened she was, I turned traitor and consciously avoided meeting her eye. The reason, of course, was that I didn't have the answers and I knew that if we caught each other's eyes, the game was up. We know each other too well. I did manage to step down with one foot and let go the gunwale long enough to give her knee a squeeze, but I bounced right back up with the kicking of the boat and didn't try it again.

I shouted, 'Two minutes! We're doing fine!' But as I couldn't see what was ahead or how far we'd come, I hadn't the faintest idea *how* we were doing.

Allan, dear love him, was playing the same game and keeping up the pretence – in his case without either the conjugal imperative of mutual support or access to a double seebackroscope – and he put his arm around Lynn's shoulders and smiled. 'Don't worry,' he said, inclining his head towards her and looking pointedly in my direction. 'Mike knows what he's doing. Fantastic little boat.' And I made an ad hoc translation – *Does Mike know what he's doing? Is it a fantastic little boat?* – which I knew I was not expected to share.

The answer to the second of these questions was an unequivocal Yes. A lesser boat, presenting her undersides again and again to a wind like that, might have been flipped or at the very least rendered unmanageably light and unstable; but her weight and the depth of her keel, together with just the right amount of sheer – the compound curves of the hull that enable her to shed wind as well as water – kept her diving and plunging ahead in more or less the right direction, and the rising pool of saltwater that sloshed around the others' sea boots could scarcely be blamed on her. She took the light from my eyes every time her bow came crashing down, but clearly while she was still on the drawing board, her designers had equipped her with just enough bow to ensure that a hand's width of freeboard would generally keep her on the right side of the surprisingly subtle dividing line between a boat and a submarine.

In the end it wasn't the bow that provided us with an experience to remember, but the stern. The With has a cutaway transom, which allows the outboard, and thus the centre of gravity, to be set as low as possible; but at the same time reduces the amount of freeboard at the stern by six inches. Inboard of the transom, and separated from the rest of the boat by an upstanding fibreglass sill, is a shallow well with a drain hole designed so that any water flowing in over the stern is trapped and duly returned to the sea. Curiously enough, though, the well is not very deep and the sill is not very high, stopping three or four inches short of the gunwales; and this combination, as we moved into an even bigger sea and the With began, like an airplane about to leave the runway, to dip her rump very low before attempting each new climb, proved to be our Achilles' heel.

Suddenly I too had water around my ankles, and Allan was pointing open-mouthed at something behind me. I twisted on the balls of my feet in time to see the backflow of what had clearly been quite a few gallons of water, running out over the transom as the With pushed valiantly upwards. As she crested, paused and began to tip forward again, the stern rose and the propeller momentarily came out of the water and gave a shriek of indignation before plunging back under and driving us down onto the next wave. When we arrived, I was thrown forward off my perch and landed at Lynn's feet, floundering like a trout in six inches of water.

Believe it or not, my first thought was that it had been a false economy not to get a waterproof pouch for my mobile; more important, without someone on the tiller, the With would come off the wind and start to turn, and even I knew that that would be a bad thing. Left to wallow side on to the waves, she would take on water very quickly over her windward side, so I scrambled up and grabbed the tiller arm, correcting a gradual slew to starboard just as the whole process was starting again.

For the second time, an unwelcome volume of water came in over the stern, and I yelled to Allan: 'Grab the baler!'

'Say again?'

'The baler!'

'Baler?'

Oh for goodness sake.

'The blue plastic thingy with the handle. We have to lose some water!'

'Okey-dokey,' he said, and all credit to him, he went right to it, relinquishing his hold on the gunwale and scooping two-litre balerfuls of water into the air in quick succession, to be whipped astern of us on the wind. It was a sterling effort, perhaps given extra potency by a wish to survive, and it meant that for the moment at least our nett intake of water was manageable; but he wouldn't be able to keep it up indefinitely and I made the decision I should have made much earlier.

'We'll go back!' I yelled. 'Keep baling if you can, we may take in a bit more water.'

I so knew that that was an understatement, and unfortunately so did Lynn. Often, crossing to the island in a moderate wind from south of west, we have taken it straight on to avoid getting wet, bypassing the cabin before turning in to the jetty with the waves at our stern. Even using the lee of the opposite shore, or the bulky hull of *Family's Pride*, the converted trawler moored off the island, to make the turn, there was often an uncomfortable moment when the boat came beam on to the waves and did a little corkscrew, allowing in enough water to give us a foretaste of what it might be like to try the same manoeuvre in a big sea.

I stole a quick glance at Lynn; smiled, chickened out and turned away again to get a fix on Dunnyneil.

'Let's have the picnic on Dunnyneil,' I shouted. 'Too bad about The Narrows!'

That sounded so fatuous I almost hoped she couldn't hear me.

I scanned ahead for a break in the waves, any piece of quieter water that might present a chance of turning more safely. Two or three little pockets materialised briefly but before I could use them they seemed to morph into something ugly and unreadable and I kept saying, 'Shoot, missed that one ... Oops! Too late, sorry!'

When the moment did come and I yanked the tiller arm towards me and held it into my ribs to make a tight turn to port, I was trusting to luck as much as to judgement. The With came obediently off the wind and there was an unreal and wholly unexpected interlude of seeming inertia as she slid sideways down the face of the next wave, stern overtaking bow with balletic fluidity, exposing the most vulnerable point of her hull – the corner where the gunwale meets the transom – to the mercy of the sea.

I experienced the moment she struck the water in much the same dreamlike way that I had experienced a bad car accident on a cliff edge above Nicola Lake in British Columbia; that is, in extreme slow motion. From BC there is an image of dark water behind a screen of sparks that flew past my head as we slid on our roof along a steel crash barrier, high above the lake; now there were bubbles, spray and white foam as the entire stern seemed to sink beneath my feet. With echoes of Jimmy Maxwell, who yelled hysterically, 'You wrecked my mother's car! You wrecked my mother's car!' over and over as we slid off the crash barrier and somersaulted back across the road, I heard Lynn shout, 'What's happening, Mike?' as the boat stalled and wallowed as if tethered to the sea bed by an unseen cable that threatened to wind us in, stern-first, below the waves.

Allan yelled, 'What can I do? Will I keep baling?'

I had never felt less like laughing but I laughed and yelled back, 'What do *you* think?' And he redoubled his already herculean efforts with the baler.

Lynn said again, 'I don't like this, Mike!'

Excellent seagoing boat that she is, the With hauled her stern out of the water by degrees and motored doggedly on, and when I looked ahead, I was overwhelmingly, almost tearfully, relieved to see that we had turned through 180 degrees and were pointing in the general direction of Dunnyneil, and safety. I doubted whether we could have taken another wave over the stern and still managed to recover. As it was, with so much water on board there was very little freeboard available, so I resisted the temptation to throttle up, and tried to hold the boat at precisely the same speed as the sea.

Lynn was pale and quiet. She suffers from seasickness at the best of times – we both do – but I sensed not only that from here on she would see expeditions in anything less than a flat calm in a very different light, but also that I had not yet heard the end of the matter of proper eye contact or the lack of it. She was right to be upset. It had been unforgivable and we both learned lessons.

As we cleared the edge of the rough water once again, Allan was able to drop the baler. He planted his elbows on his knees and lowered his head with exhaustion. I could see water or sweat, or both, dripping from his nose but I couldn't make out the expression on his face. No one said anything for quite a time; then I heard a kind of thin chant, the same singsong words repeated again and again and rising steadily in volume. Allan is a deeply religious person and at first I thought he might be giving thanks, but when he raised his head he was looking sideways at Lynn and grinning, and I realised that religion had nothing to do with it.

'I don't like this, Mike. *I don't like this*!' he was saying, with obvious relish, and Lynn half-grinned and said: 'Well ...!'

Later, in the visitors' book, Allan painted a view of the sound with a dark sky and an edgy-looking sea; and below that, under the heading

'A Few Things to Observe', he added a list of pointers for future guests, including this:

They will try to take you to a place called PORT-A-SCARY. Beware ... A near death experience awaits.

turquoise boat. yellow man

Eighteen

On the last morning of Allan's stay he made two watercolour sketches of the dogs. Rab is lying on the living-room window seat with his head on a cushion, gazing lopsidedly towards the mainland, and Jock is fast asleep in a patch of sun on the veranda.

Lynn loves the veranda. She goes on a bit about it, particularly to visitors arriving on cold days in winter, or wet days in any season; as in the hopelessly wishful, 'It's hard to believe we had coffee on the veranda yesterday', or the unrealistically hopeful, 'With any luck we'll have coffee on the veranda tomorrow.' But it does reflect the fact that, weather permitting, the veranda is the base of operations for much of our existence on the island.

Obviously, as you have to walk across it to get to the front door and along it to get to the bathroom, you can't ignore it, but because of the cabin's location, the veranda probably sees as much day-to-day living as the living room. One of the first things we did when we arrived was to sacrifice shelter, and to some extent privacy, for a view by strategically removing sections of weatherboarding from the balustrade at the edge of the veranda, and fitting open rails so that wherever we sat we could see the foreshore as well as the water. It was what we had tried to achieve with the farmhouse in Kinross-shire: breathing space and some sense of being a part of the world beyond the walls.

At one end there is a cross-legged dining table with benches, and at the other, a pair of rustic garden seats and a coffee table, which Lynn and I knocked up from lengths of mismatched scrap wood one fairly comedic afternoon in December. Tucked into a corner next to the coffee table is an outdoor gas heater, clad with timber and painted the same New England blue as the cabin – Valtti, the paint manufacturers, have helpfully recorded the formula in their Edinburgh depot under the name Island Blue – by means of which we have often managed to extend the length of a veranda day from sunrise to well after dark.

Hinged onto the balustrade is a little fold-away two-seater table of my own design, which has never, to my recollection, been folded away and to which we are drawn at meal times on lazy Sundays to sit with the water at our elbows.

Breakfast: fried eggs on croissants with chipotle chile. Coffee: fresh

ground continental from Braithwaite's of Dundee. Lunch: Adamson's of Pittenweem oatcakes with Cashel blue and Lynn's date and onion chutney – the world's finest. Dinner (candlelit): wheaten bread, rocket salad and roasted tomatoes with parmesan shavings. The wheaten bread, as well as a kind of Irish stew derivative, are my only regular contributions to the table, my excuse being that Lynn loves to cook. The bread is to my mother's recipe but I'm proud to say I developed the stew myself while sharing a flat with five other students at Aberdeen university. The hitherto secret ingredients haven't changed much and are what you might expect to find in a flat full of gastronomically challenged male undergraduates: any kind of meat; potatoes, carrots, onions and tomatoes – the only vegetables known to me at the time; every conceivable sauce, including red, brown, Worcester, HP, and the ubiquitous soy; curry paste, mango chutney and on at least one occasion Thousand Island dressing; and of course copious quantities of dried mixed spice, something you wouldn't find in Lynn's kitchen, even buried at the back of a drawer. It all went in at the same time and was judged to be ready when enough of it had become permanently attached to the pan.

The veranda runs like a coloured thread through photographs of island life from thirty years ago. There are several taken from the jetty, which show the family in various states of partial undress or in swimming gear, reading on the wooden steps, sunbathing on multicoloured trifold plastic and aluminium loungers, which were classics of the period and used to collapse without warning; or fiddling at sheets and stays on the Mirror dinghy, which lived on the grass in front of the veranda when it wasn't in the water.

Before we had a mains water supply, and on the pretext of hygiene, my father used to wake us every morning by running along the veranda in his swimming trunks, clapping his hands and shouting, 'Everybody up! Swim before breakfast!' It was a never-failing and sometimes dreaded ritual from which there was no escape. Da was always first in, closely followed by Claire, but you had to be fast to witness it. He would wade up to his knees on the jetty, hugging himself, beating his chest with clenched fists and making chimplike *oo oh oh* sounds. Then he would bend at the knees and take a great leap, his arms doing a high speed breaststroke before he even hit the water. Once in, it was a dozen breathless strokes in a tight circle and back to the jetty. All over in ten seconds. Claire followed a similar routine but with the insane refinement of a prolonged pause while she crouched in the water up to her neck before the big leap. Early in the season, before the water temperature had risen to almost tolerable levels, it was quite a trial, but consistent with the Faulkner tradition of all for one, one for all, we would grit our teeth and submit to our saltwater bath, until eventually it was taken for granted – even, on occasion, enjoyed. The only person who ever escaped was my mother, who discovered that getting bacon and eggs on the go would sometimes qualify her for ad hoc exemption at our combined discretion.

Inevitably passers-by in boats, unaware they could be heard, would make comments when they spotted my father on the veranda. 'Would you look at the old b——r sunning himself?' was not unknown, though much less likely than the more affectionate 'There's wee Brian!' It's a common misconception, especially with people used to the noise-clutter of life around traffic, buildings and, I suppose, other people, that sound behaves in the same way everywhere, even surrounded by water in the middle of nowhere. It's a big assumption and it can end in tears, because in fact the fag ends of a casual conversation on the water can be picked up and pieced together half a mile or more downwind.

With years of experience handling hecklers at politically heated constituency meetings, my father's automatic response to all such petty intrusions was a smile and a wave; but on one glorious occasion the hand of fate reached out on his behalf and dealt a passing motorboat and its unsuspecting passengers an eloquent and exquisitely timed dose of poetic justice. Just off the end of the jetty and a little to the south there is a large crescent-shaped rock whose presence is only ever betrayed at dead low-water, when curling blade-ends of brown oarweed break the surface. The Admiralty chart, while it doesn't outline the rock as such, gives the low-water depth as .6 m, so a prudent helmsman has no excuse for hitting it; but over the years we have seen dozens of boats ride up its slope, bounce clear over it, strike it a glancing blow or simply stop dead in the water with a thud, and keel over – helpless, perhaps damaged but certainly, and worst of all, highly embarrassed. Even on a rising tide it can be an hour before there is enough water to refloat; on a falling tide the wait can be a mortifying three hours or more.

My mother used to try to signal a warning by waving her arms and pointing at the rock, but the response was either to wave back in a friendly manner or pointedly to ignore her, as if to say, 'Blooming cheek, we have as much right to be here as ...' *Crrunch*. Warnings rarely worked and for the hapless sailors at whom they were directed they probably made the long minutes that followed even more excruciating, as they struggled to hold on to their dignity at an undignified angle of 45 degrees.

On this particular occasion, the boat was a fast and expensive-looking motor cruiser, a downsize version of the type seen parked stern first against the marina in Saint-Tropez. A group of five or six men were standing on the flying bridge with glasses in their hands, looking in our direction. Someone pointed and we couldn't hear what was said but the tone was clear enough, and it wasn't friendly. They were travelling south, which normally means that due to a gentle slope on the north face of the rock, the impact is less severe, but they were doing a good speed and the tide was at its very lowest.

We all looked at one another with expectant grimaces, and David, who unlike the rest of us knew the precise location of the rock, stood up for a better view, leaning his elbows on the balustrade. Barely moving his lips and with all the nonchalance he could muster, he said quietly, 'Wait for it. Wait for it!' and moments later there was a series of hollow thuds and the boat rose slowly out of the water, turned sharply to port and basically fell over; crashed, as it were, on takeoff. Lying almost on her side, she must nevertheless have found her point of balance because she rocked gently to and fro for a few moments, pirouetted ever so gracefully anticlockwise until she came face on to the cabin (albeit pointing somewhere into the treetops behind us) and then just as gracefully slid backwards off the rock and into deeper water – saved, one would hope, by the weight of bodies dumped off her flying bridge and piled haphazardly into the open cockpit at her stern.

Her name, as with so many Strangford boats, was Something *of Cuan*. Pride, perhaps.

Boat names have come to hold something of a sad fascination for me. If David can tell you the displacement, length overall and sailing characteristics of a given boat, I can tell you her name. Not as sad, perhaps, as train-, plane- or truck-spotting, because the names are prettier and often tell you something of the history of the boat or her owners, but even so I don't often talk about this interest with my friends. What first struck me was how inventive people can be, particularly if they have large families, in badging their beloved boats with the names of their beloved children. There is a yacht called *Tandara*, for example, which lies off the pontoons; I don't know her owners well but I won't be surprised to find there have been three children called Tania, David and Rachel. Another has been anagrammatically christened *Yarrum* to take in the entire family: their name is Murray. And in the picture postcard harbour of Lynn's home town of Pittenweem in Fife, when the fishing fleet is in, the boats' names provide a veritable who's who of the female (always female, in accordance with superstition) progeny of generations of local fishermen; some are so pretty that you wonder if siblings have been christened according to the poetic potential of their combined and truncated names. My favourite, *Shalona*, which used to fish out of Anstruther, just along the coast, immortalised three sisters from a well-known East Neuk fishing family: Sheena, Alison and Fiona Gardiner.

Only having been blessed with a four-legged family of our own, if we ever have a proper boat, we shall name her *Rajo*.

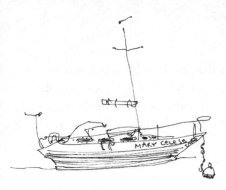

Nineteen

One yacht at Ringhaddy is so spookily and, as it turns out, aptly named that she drifts into my dreams occasionally, looming large but immaterial out of the gloom.

On a mild and very still evening in early March Lynn and I took the With to the north end of the sound for dinner with my uncle. His house, low-profiled and splashed with ivy, is uniquely sited in the shadow of a ruined Elizabethan castle at the neck of a tree-studded headland, tellingly named Castle Island. The isthmus on which the house stands is so narrow that the tide rises towards the front and back doors simultaneously, and it's easy to see why the castle was built in such a place, having all the defensive advantages of an island with the convenience of a permanent umbilical to the mainland proper. After dinner, Uncle Dennis came as far as the stone jetty in front of the house to see us off. The castle walls rose with quiet splendour above us, palely reflecting the lights of the house, and the air was so heavy with the musky scent of damp seaweed that I could taste salt on my lips.

We poled away into the darkness and dropped the outboard. I was about to pull the starter cord when I saw Uncle Dennis looking out over the sound towards the south. He was saying something quietly, as though to himself, and I paused in mid-pull.

'Sorry?'

He shrugged.

'Feels like fog,' he said. 'Just as well you didn't leave it any later.'

I looked around, and so did Lynn, and it didn't feel a bit like fog.

It was moonless, dank and unusually dark but I could make out at least a couple of mooring buoys close to, and I didn't see any problem with navigating home as long as we went carefully. On the other hand, my uncle has been around boats and the sea all his life, and if he makes comment on either one, it's wise to listen.

'We'll go easy,' I said. 'Thanks.'

'Safe home,' he said.

It hadn't occurred to me before, but there was something about his profile, outlined against the lights of the house, that reminded me of my father, and I felt a little rush of affection. The unmistakable Faulkner carriage, on or off a horse.

I started the motor and we waved and puttered off into mid-channel – to be utterly enveloped by an advancing wall of the thickest fog I have ever experienced. One moment I was checking out the sound for boats and buoys, and the next I could see Lynn sitting next to me and nothing else. I couldn't make out the other end of the boat. We were only 150 yards from shore, in a waterway I thought I knew like the back of my hand, and suddenly I understood every sailor's nightmare. There was no way of knowing how fast we were going or quite where we were in relation to anything else on, or under, the water. Even so, I had the absurd notion that I was roughly aware of our heading, and that if we continued straight on, we would strike the far side of the sound and could simply turn right, hugging the shore of Islandmore and eventually, inevitably, arriving back at our own jetty.

I ran this thought past Lynn, whose sense of direction is more reliable than mine, and she said reassuringly: 'I have no idea what direction we're going. How can you tell? Besides, how will we know when we're close to shore? What if we hit a rock going in?'

Far too many questions.

'What do you suggest?' I said.

'How about lifting the outboard and rowing.'

'What, all the way?'

'No, just to the shore. If you're right, we're bound to end up on Islandmore. We can walk home and come back for the boat in the morning.'

That was, in fact, the most logical – and the safest – plan. But the With is not easy to row and I compromised by releasing the lock on the outboard so that I could lift the propeller out of the water at a moment's notice. I throttled back until we were making minimum speed, and every few seconds I tried to slow the boat down still further by engaging neutral and allowing her to cruise.

Lynn disappeared in the direction of the bow, to keep a lookout and hopefully to fend off on anything big and solid she might meet up there: in wintertime there are only thirty or forty boats in the sound (though upwards of two hundred moorings), but at that moment every one of them was somewhere between us and the cabin.

Several long minutes of stop-start progress went by, and for all we encountered we might have been a small speck on a vast and featureless ocean many miles from home. We saw nothing, touched nothing, and soon the same nagging thought came into both our minds: it was conceivable that by chance we might have avoided all those boats and moorings scattered around us, but a body of land three-quarters of a mile wide was another matter. Where on earth was Islandmore?

The fact that we had not picked up weed or grounded on the island's bouldered shore proved only that we could be anywhere, even leaving the sound altogether via the narrow channel between Islandmore and Dunsy, our nearest neighbour to the north. There are many things in Ringhaddy Sound which no one would wish to hit, like the two stone quays or the steel bulk of *Splendour*, a Toronto-registered motor cruiser; but either would be preferable to the rocks that lurked beyond the cosy confines of the sound – Gull, Sand, Hadd, James, Pawle, Dunsy or Strife. Especially Strife.

I decided to cut the outboard after all, and row. I dropped in the rowlocks but before seating the first oar I drove the blade end into the water as far as I could to see if it hit the bottom. It didn't. Wherever we were, we were in more than eight feet of water.

Lynn said, 'Can you see anything?'

'I can't even see you. How about you?'

'Nothing. This is unreal.'

The absence of normal points of reference did indeed give the whole thing an air of unreality. Our disembodied voices seemed amplified by the stillness, and there was an odd sensory contrast between the womblike embrace of the fog and the blind vulnerability of the boat. It was more unsettling than frightening, for me at least, but it was early days.

As we had started off by taking a right-handed diagonal across the sound, I reasoned that we were more likely to have veered inadvertently to right than to left, and that Islandmore must be somewhere off our port bow. In that case, if we did run ashore, I would feel the gloopy resistance of seaweed on the right oar first; a helpful early warning, to which, putting it mildly, I greatly looked forward.

Sure enough, after a few dozen laboured strokes with the With's outsized and rather unwieldy oars, something grabbed one of the blades and held on. There being much more oar outside the boat than in, leverage tends to be on the side of the weed and I responded by digging in with the opposite oar to slow us down. The only thing was, the weed had taken hold of the wrong oar – the left one – and the implication of *that* was that we had either recrossed the sound and arrived back on the mainland, which would be unhelpful, or that we had managed to about-turn and were following the western shoreline of Islandmore or Dunsy northwards and away from home. It was all very confusing but at least we had arrived *somewhere*, and to find out where, I stood up and started to pole my way carefully into the shallows.

Lynn's voice came from the bow in a tense whisper: 'Did you hear that?'

'It's just the oar on the bottom,' I said. 'I'm poling in.'

'No,' she said. 'Out behind us.'

I listened hard. At first there was nothing and then I heard the telltale *clink*, half-hearted but unmistakable, of steel rigging against an aluminium mast. Whatever yacht was out there, she was very close and we had disturbed the glassy surface of the water in such a way as to set her on a slight sway. Twice more she sent her gentle morse call in our direction, and then fell silent.

A thought occurred to me, a plan that might save us a good deal of walking or rowing.

'Let's see who she is,' I said. 'She might just get us home.'

My idea was that if I recognised the name of the yacht, we would know our position; and that given the state of the tide (not long on the ebb), her disposition would also suggest the direction of the cabin: she would be lying north–south, so our jetty should be somewhere along an imaginary line off her stern and a little to the east.

My interest in boat names was about to come into its own. The risk, obviously, was that given our recent record, we might not be able to find the mystery yacht, but we decided to give it a go and while I set up to row, Lynn positioned herself on the bench seat in front of me and tried to keep a fix on the spot that was her best guess as to the source of the sound.

Now that we could see each other we were able to work as a team. Lynn pointed, and I took a few strokes with one oar until the With was in line with her outstretched arm. Then I rowed as gently and noiselessly as I could, making little adjustments in accordance with my human compass, ready to dig in with both oars the moment a dead stop was called for.

But after a few minutes, we began to lose heart. Lynn shook her head and dropped her arm to her side, and I lifted the oars clear of the water and allowed the boat to drift. Our little gamble, it seemed, hadn't paid off but Lynn was philosophical.

'Needle in a hay stack, I suppose,' she said.

I thought: Thirty or forty feet of needle. We really shouldn't have missed her. I didn't say anything but I felt a bit wretched that it had been my idea to head off again into the unknown. Had we gone ashore at least we would have learnt where we were, for better or worse.

We sat in sullen silence, drifting with the ebb tide; making, probably, two or three knots in a more or less southerly direction. It was cooler now and Lynn zipped up her oilskins and drew her knees up to her chest. I was watching her, feeling increasingly guilty and wondering what to do next when she sat bolt upright and fixed her eyes on something behind me.

'You're not going to believe this,' she said.

As I turned, a dark and phantasmal *something* was closing on our starboard bow. It reared above us, with no discernible form, but around eye level and only feet away, a tidy row of white letters spelt out a familiar name; and the name, without a word of a lie, was *Mary Celeste*.

I shuddered. *Mary Celeste* might be one of the prettier yachts in the sound but that, if anything, had always made the choice of name all the more intriguing.

'Of all the boats ...' I said to Lynn. 'A good thing we're not superstitious.'

'*You're* not superstitious,' she said, but I could see that she was just as relieved as I was.

I knew that *Mary Celeste* lay off Islandmore at the mouth of the first bay north of the cabin, and she obligingly gave us not just a route home, but a pretty clear insight into our journey so far. It would appear that without realising it we had passed close by her already, deftly avoiding not just her but every other boat on the water as we zigzagged down the length of the sound. We must have crossed the open mouth of the bay and veered somewhat left before striking its southern shore. That would explain why the left oar had found the shallows first and also why the sound of *Mary Celeste*'s rigging had seemed, as Lynn had thought at the time, to come from behind us.

In less than ten minutes we were on the jetty, and it is the only occasion, not wanting to venture even fifty yards into the sound, that I have ever deliberately bypassed the rowing boat and left it where it was on the mooring, tied the With to the jetty and allowed her to dry out on the stones and shingle with the falling tide.

Such, I suppose I could always claim, was my new-found respect for the elements.

Twenty

Goodbye, amore, Islandmore, we'll be back for more and more –
Thank-you so much, you picnic King and Queen.
Sean & Christine xx

I got the picnic habit at quite an early age – perhaps three or four. By and large, memories from that time run only to snapshot images, or series of images, but just to prove the rule, I do have a very vivid recollection of being swung up onto Nimrod, a big grey hunter, by my father. He got me to hold on to the saddle with both hands, and led me in a little circuit of the back paddock. The others are sitting together on the grass, smiling up at me from far below. My mother is clapping. She is flanked on one side by David and Claire, and on the other by Winnie Wilson, our nanny and lifelong friend. Winnie has a big basket balanced on her knees.

Perhaps it's a composite memory but that little sequence, played out again and again with the same cast of characters and variations only as to place – the meet after a day's hunting, long after everyone else has gone home; Tyrella beach on New Year's Day; the grassy bank beside the high jump at Mourne Grange – has in it all the constants of my childhood: picnic baskets, fresh air, family and horses.

As for Lynn and me, from the picnic point of view our life courses converged with poetic inevitability. As one of six children spanning fourteen years, she found herself making her own amusement more often than I did. For her, doing everything 'as a family' would probably have seemed bizarre, and with raw materials at her disposal

like intertidal pools, sandy coves and fingers of volcanic rock reaching
into the Firth of Forth from the beach, it doesn't surprise me that the
solitary side of her nature took her deep within the shadows of
overhanging skellies and into sandy crevices clutching baked beans, an
egg or two, discarded tin cans and bits of driftwood for a fire. In this
secret world she would spend hours brewing up, crushing coloured
stones and adding seawater to make a rudimentary clay, from which
she formed bowls, using rounded stone indentations as moulds. She
couldn't use these creations, or even move them, and she was happy
to give them to the tide. Others only ever saw them by accident and
in that sense they anticipated the integrity of her later work: art, as it
were, for art's sake.

Her picnic fare is more sophisticated now, but the impulse hasn't
changed and happily she has been prepared to budge up and make
room for me. We picnicked our way through our first island winter in
all conditions and in every quarter of the lough, dragging our bemused
guests with us.

We introduced my friend and lawyer, Dale, and his girlfriend,
Trish, to boats, reckless adventure, and extreme picnicking, all in the
course of one March weekend. I knew by his horrified reaction when
I pulled the rowing boat up the jetty a little and unscrewed the sea
bung to let out some water ('It has a *plug*?!') that Dale hadn't been
around boats much, so I should have known better than to make our

first expedition a picnic on the windward side of Pawle.

Pawle Island lies behind Islandmore, separated from it by a shallow sound, which is safely navigable only at half-tide or over. A faded and rather quaint throwback to a more optimistic era of pre-war island agriculture, Pawle is partly encircled by a neat stone wall studded with traditional County Down gateposts – round, with dull points, like the stumps of well-used crayons – which used to be hung with wrought-iron gates. Near the southwest corner, in its own walled enclosure and surrounded by trees, is the dilapidated shell of a handsome nineteenth-century farmhouse. It was last lived in around 1960 and is currently tenanted, on and off, by a flock of semi-wild, long-haired white goats who use every room in the house when they are in residence, including the upstairs bedrooms. I always have the nagging feeling, when I stand in the half-dark under the trees and look up at the glassless windows, that the goats are not alone, and that one day a voice from within will answer my unspoken greeting.

> 'Is there anybody there?' said the traveller,
> Knocking on the moonlit door;
> And his horse in the silence champed the grasses
> Of the forest's ferny floor.

On the foreshore in front of the old house, facing Pawle Sound and Islandmore, are the remains of a cobbled landing slip. Not really remains, because like everything else on Pawle, the slip appears to have been soundly built with a view to permanence, and no doubt beneath the silt and the shingle, which have all but engulfed it, it will still be largely intact. At one time, while its western edge would have blended, as today, into the rocks of the foreshore, at the opposite edge, away from the prevailing wind, a channel deep enough for flatboats might have run along the side of a vertical wall.

The slip is somewhat exposed to a westerly or northwesterly wind but there isn't too much weed. When we decided, at breakfast, to take Dale and Trish to Pawle for lunch, the sun was out, the sky was clear from horizon to horizon and the breeze, albeit from the west, was light. Remarkably for the time of year, it was warm enough to use the veranda and we sat around all morning, catching up.

It was good to see Dale. We became friendly twenty years ago when I was asked to show him round the firm where I was serving my legal apprenticeship. A year ahead of me in the profession, Dale was joining the firm at the relatively exalted level of legal assistant, but for a couple of hours I was in charge and I took him on an extended tour of the premises, at that time something of a rabbit warren, knocking on doors and introducing him to people I didn't know myself, more or less at random. I contrived several times to cross the landing where the coffee machine lived, adding in the process a good half-hour to my unexpected exeat from the filing room, deep within the bowels of the building, where I had spent a fortnight at a big rectangular table piled high with miscellaneous papers and correspondence, in some cases going back years, for which it was my exciting task to find homes among the banks of six-drawer filing cabinets lining the room.

I even took Dale down to the typing pool, whose very whereabouts was apparently a mystery to more than a few lawyers in the building, and introduced him to the girls there en masse. I like to think that my endorsement of this energetic, ginger-haired new boy, whose talent has since taken him inexorably up through the ranks of the profession, made a significant difference to the speed at which his carefully dictated words of legal advice made it back to his desk thereafter, because I had recently won an informal vote for Dictator of the Year by the same typing pool — nothing frustrates a typist more than sloppy dictation — an achievement that gave me as much satisfaction as my law degree.

As we got ready to leave for Pawle, Lynn spotted a darkening sky to the southwest and insisted we take oilskins. The wind was getting up too, but the cabin was still in sunshine, lulling us — me — into a false sense of security as we pushed off from the jetty. When we left one sound and turned the point of Islandmore into the other, I could see that there was a good sea running onto the landing on Pawle; but not really having experienced the difficulties of landing on a windward shore, I put the boat in anyway.

We got into trouble almost immediately. When I lifted the outboard in the shallows, we didn't drift in quietly as intended; we shot in at some speed and I grabbed the oars and gave one to Dale.

'Better slow us down a bit!' I said, forcing Dale, in the absence of clearer instructions, simply to copy me as best he could as I thrust the oar into the water ahead of us and tried to get a purchase on the cobbles.

The With did slow down, but only to the extent that the inevitable impact came more as a series of little thuds than one big crash, and then we were being lifted and dumped, lifted and dumped in an alarming, unseamanlike and highly embarrassing manner, with no chance whatsoever, as things stood, of returning to deeper water.

Lynn vaulted over the bow with the rope in her hand and splashed ashore.

'You go too, Trish!' I said, less calmly than I hoped. 'Take the food, we won't be able to hang around with the boat.'

That came out all wrong, but Trish was laughing as she grabbed the basket and followed Lynn.

'Going to leave us here, are you?' she said over her shoulder.

'We shall return!' I said solemnly; but first we had to figure out how to leave.

I lowered Rab, who enjoys swimming, over the side of the boat and he followed the girls ashore. Lynn came back for Jock, a year and a half Rab's senior and much too old and wise for this kind of thing. She reached over the gunwale and swept him up into her arms, cradling him close as she picked her way back through the surf, and depositing him gently on the shingle.

I found myself having to shout over the wind: 'Chuck back the rope, this is pointless!'

I turned to Dale. He was leaning on the oar and managing to take some of the sting out of the jolting each time the boat bottomed out. He raised his eyebrows and cocked his head. 'Now what?' he said, instinctively assuming, I think, that however things might turn out, his place, now that women and dogs had abandoned ship, was in the boat with me, shoulder to shoulder, doing rescue stuff.

I had other plans for him, though. By now the With was hard aground but with some of her human ballast off-loaded I was sure our chances of getting her off again had improved. I rummaged in the stern locker for a length of polypropylene rope, tied one end to the little collapsible anchor that my brother, with great prescience, had suggested I keep in the boat for such occasions; tied the other end to the bow rope Lynn had thrown to me, and seated the rowlocks. Then I laid in the oars and jammed their heels together in the bow of the boat. Set up in this way, ready for action, the blade ends splayed upwards and outwards from the rowlocks in mute supplication to the strengthening wind, but without result: it blew all the harder, and as if on cue, the bank of dark cloud Lynn had seen earlier arrived and brought with it a cold and drenching rain.

The first problem was how to turn the boat round so that her bow was into the wind.

'Would you mind stepping out and turning the boat round, Dale?' I shouted, very politely, as one would shout to one's solicitor. 'I'll give you a hand.'

I retrieved one of the oars and Dale launched himself co-operatively over the side and put his shoulder to the bow of the boat. He must have been standing in two or three feet of water. I moved my weight to the opposite side to get the With off her keel and make use of the flotation of her rounded hull, at the same time digging in with the oar. She came round sluggishly and as soon as she was pointing more or less to windward I dropped the oar back into the rowlock, hefted the anchor and flung it as far as I could into the mud-bottomed channel of Pawle Sound. I managed a respectable distance and began pulling on the rope, at which point Dale, about whom I had temporarily forgotten, yelled from behind.

'What about me!'

'Give her a really good shove,' I said. 'Best stay with the others, she isn't the lightest boat to row.'

Dale gave me a good start and I continued to pull hand over hand on the rope. As soon as I was clear of the weed I intended to row far enough out to give myself time to drop the outboard before I was driven in again by the wind. It was a sound plan and it was working quite well until the moment the rope went slack, and I learned a valuable lesson about polypropylene rope: if you're tying off to an anchor, use a double bowline, or a water bowline, or better still an anchor hitch, because otherwise it's liable to work loose if the load is taken off, even for a moment, and eventually fail.

Left kneeling in the bow with nothing to pull on, I said a bad word and looked back at Dale, feeling foolish and not really looking forward to doing the whole thing over again. He may have had the same thoughts – may even have said the same word – because he started making rowing motions with his arms, and I obliged by diving onto the centre thwart and grabbing the oars. I was halfway back to shore but not yet in the heaviest weed, and I began rowing with a ferociousness that surprised me and no doubt impressed the others. I was better than holding my own, increasing the distance between us by inches, and once I had started, lest I should hear the words *another fine mess* from any of the three of them, I refused to let up. With short, steep strokes, I managed to get the edge on the wind, and choosing my moment, I let go the oars and scrambled to the stern, simultaneously dropping the outboard, pulling the start cord and saying a quiet prayer. I don't often pray and when I do, I tend to use my brother's childhood version of the Lord's Prayer, on the basis that it might, in a crisis, appeal to His sense of humour. 'For Thine is the kingdom, the car and the lorry,' I whispered, and the motor responded by firing on the first pull.

I pulled away at some speed, and turned a wide circle in the middle of Pawle Sound. Looking back through the driving rain at the little group standing on the foreshore – a forlorn, still and strangely picturesque tableau – it occurred to me that although, as usual, I had left mine at home, one of them probably had a mobile and I made phone signals, holding my right hand against my ear. Dale acknowledged by giving an exaggerated thumbs up and reaching into his pocket, and just to confuse him I headed off in the direction of Islandmore and left them to ponder their chances of survival should I fail to return: *four rolls, three people, two dogs; three weeks?*

As soon as I got to the jetty I retrieved my mobile and called Dale. I told him I would collect them from the lee side of the island in ten minutes, where the wind would be less strong and, crucially, in our favour. He said, 'Fine', and apparently after signing off, he turned to Lynn and said: 'We're meeting Mike on the lee side. Where's that then?'

Having left Pawle Island in the rain, by the time I returned the sun was shining and we decided to have our picnic after all. We found a sheltered bank above an unusually sandy bay, where the With could lie in deep water on a long line, and we sat down in our oilskins, business as usual. The rolls were cheese and chorizo salad with mayonnaise and basil leaves, the wine was a choice of Pinot Grigio or Merlot, and Lynn had brought along real coffee in a flask. Given the experience of the last hour, it was the picnic of picnics, and to cap it all, another, somewhat greyer, cloud came our way and gave us an unremitting and wholly unexpected ten minutes worth, not of rain, but of hail.

As hailstones bounced off her plate and filled up the little crease above the peak of her oilskin hood, Trish said, with feeling: 'This is fun!'

Twenty-one

Paradoxically, a double dose of her blacker moods – the fury and the fog – seemed only to bring me closer to the lough.

Taking advantage of the fact that my mental time-clock is out of sync with Lynn's by around an hour and a half, come spring I took to filling a flask and heading out of the sound in the early morning for the simple pleasure of pottering about in the boat and exploring.

Tide permitting, a handful of brent geese would be grazing the tide-line in front of the cabin. When they first arrived in the last week of March, attracted by the first green shoots of slitch, an algae-like weed they seem to enjoy, they would take to the water as soon I came down the steps from the veranda, swimming in formation into the sound; but by mid-April the geese, like the heron, had learned to ignore me even as I walked down the jetty and rowed past them to the mooring. I would pause to watch, enjoying their company while it lasted – they would be gone by the end of the month, bound for Greenland and Spitsbergen to breed.

Normally, to avoid the anchorage and civilisation, I would exit the sound to the south and motor the length of Pawle Sound on my way to the open lough. Through April and May the grass of the islands thickens quickly and turns a rich and luxurious green, outpacing the sheep in their efforts to graze it down; and the thorn hedges burst out of themselves in a snowy extravagance of spring blossom. The odd fox, emboldened by the relative safety of his insular habitat, will cross the open spaces between them with casual impunity, stopping to stare at the boat for a few moments before going on his relaxed, unhurried way.

On the lookout for waders and waterfowl, I would trace the loops and whorls of the island's convoluted shoreline, making occasional landings to investigate the more promising bits of seaborne detritus, which get deposited at intervals along the high-water line. I have been known to turn up back at the cabin, not always to much obvious enthusiasm from Lynn, with a wide range of useful articles found in this way: ancient mud-filled bottles; lengths of blue polypropylene rope so encrusted and enmeshed in sun-hardened seaweed they could be stood on end; numerous buoys and pot floats in an infinite range of tones and sizes but only one colour – orange; a baffling collection of oars, some of which must have had a story to tell; and even more baffling, on one occasion a single paddle belonging to an open, Canadian-style canoe, which raised all kinds of unanswerable questions. Who were they? If there were two of them in the canoe, why did they feel the need to abandon the second paddle? If only one, how did he or she get home?

If I was on the water, as another lawyer friend used to say, at crack of sparrow, I might be lucky enough to catch a spectacle normally denied us at the cabin by the presence of Eagle Hill to the east: sunrise over the soft grey horizon of the Ards peninsula. Viewed from the sea-level perspective of a small boat and projected onto a mackerel sky in a range of colours from palest gold to blood orange, sunrise over Strangford has the silent magnificence of Notre Dame before the tourists are up, or a stand of California redwoods at dusk.

One of my early morning expeditions in May brought me to Long Sheelah, a thin sliver of shells and polished pebbles the length of a football field and the width, at mean high-water, of a medium-sized boat, which lies near the dead centre of the lough. The tapered ends of Long Sheelah's serpentine body are marked by a pair of poles, since in the highest tides it lies just a few feet below the water. I landed on the leeward side of the little island, buried the anchor in the ever-moving stony shell of its exposed back and pushed the *With* off to lie on a long line to the north.

I was looking for some descriptive background for a short story on which I was working, set on a pebbly river island in the Appalachians, and I sat down and tried to dislocate Long Sheelah in my mind's eye and transport it to the midstream of a fast-flowing, treacherous river at the bottom of an aspen-covered ravine in the unmapped vastness of early nineteenth-century American wilderness. It wasn't easy: all was open, serene and far from treacherous, and I kept being distracted by the unreadable antics of a small turquoise fishing boat half a mile away to the northeast, which was manoeuvring with complex deliberation onto the exact spots from which to drop its complement of creels.

I managed a few pages of useful revision, trudged up and down to study the sound made by rounded stones as they move and roll and slide over one another – something between a *crunch* and a *clack* – and crouched by the lough's edge to examine the refractive effect of light as it passes through water and appears to kink the line of slope.

From the constant milling action of small stones on its exposed shores, Long Sheelah is the best place on the lough to find the bleached, eroded remains of limpet shells, which have been rolled and crushed until the oldest and softest part, the crown, has disappeared altogether, leaving just the tough outer rim intact. Lynn has boxes of them on the island and strings them together to make wind chimes of the subtlest, most sleep-inducing timbre, hanging them outside the bedroom window on her beloved veranda.

I filled my pockets with shells and ended up spending far longer than intended on Long Sheelah. On the way home, aware that Lynn prefers to have a rough idea of my plans when I am on my own on the lough, I felt a pang of guilt and stopped off on the southernmost tip of Islandmore, where an impenetrable thorn hedge just above the high-water line hides a secret in its shadow. I tied the With by a slip knot to a fistful of bladder weed and scrambled across the boulders and round to the back of the hedge. There, for just a few weeks in late spring, in the corner of a damp and reedy meadow, a scattering of deep yellow flower heads worthy of Wordsworth flutters and dances in the breeze. More transient and much shyer than daffodils, the island's modest annual crop of flag irises lives and dies, for the most part, in glorious isolation, happily uncelebrated and all the more precious for that.

In the island equivalent of stopping off at a flower stall en route

from the office to the car park – something I actually wouldn't dream of doing, even when I was a lawyer – I took a single flower and a pair of its broad, enwrapping leaves and presented them to Lynn back at the cabin. She found a suitable bottle (possibly salvaged from the foreshore on an earlier expedition), and such is the yellow flag's cheerful and charismatic presence that it felt as though three of us sat down that morning to breakfast at the little foldout table. The flower bobbed and nodded between us by way of introduction, its head self-effacingly inclined. It smiled the smile of young summer.

'Passing through?' it said. 'Me too. How wonderful. Lovely day.'

It was all something of a contrast, in terms of serenity, to breakfast less than a week later.

Our guest for the weekend was Jo Steverlynck, a larger-than-life and much-loved family friend from Belgium whose heavily accented English is delivered at a volume reflecting his natural *joie de vivre*. Nothing wrong with that, but during a brief spell of sunshine on the Saturday afternoon, I took Jo on a guided tour of the area by boat. We headed south, out of the sheltered confines of Ringhaddy Sound and into the lough proper, where we cut the outboard and spent a rewarding ten minutes drifting on a gentle swell and watching the seals and guillemots go about their business.

There was scarcely a sound; only the hollow *schlapp* of water against the fibreglass hull. I handed the binoculars to Jo and leaned back against the transom on one elbow while he searched the water line on Dunsy Rock for basking seals. For a man who likes to talk, he fell unusually silent, lost in concentration. A minute passed and I turned my face to the sun and closed my eyes. This was the life.

A sharp clap from the direction of the bow, as of a gunshot, snapped me out of it. I was bolt upright, blinking hard, half-blind and disoriented. I reached behind me to grab the transom and missed, up-ending and all but disappearing over the stern. An appalling picture flashed across my mind of treading water while Jo, who as far as I know had never been *in* a small boat before, let alone driven one, started the outboard and sped round in ever-decreasing circles in a valiant rescue attempt, dicing me with the propeller into ever-thinner slices on each pass with his customary Gallic gusto.

By the time a second, and then a third bang followed, I had composed myself. Jo was clapping his big hands together with childlike exuberance.

'Ha! Yes!' he boomed.

He was looking around him, shaking his head, a smile of perfect contentment lighting his face.

'Yes yes! UN-believable! What a day. We are the lucky ones, my friend, yes?'

Well yes; my racing pulse aside, I had to agree.

We headed home as the day began to go, and re-entered the sound from the north, having meandered all the way round the island. As we threaded our way through the motor sailers, yachts and fishing boats moored in the shelter of the sound, I saw James McFerran's barge drawing away from the old quay off to our right, under tow and en route to Islandmore with a cargo of sheep. I gave way, easing off to pass to stern of him, and we exchanged waves.

Sheep do well on Islandmore, even in winter. The hedges that crisscross the low rises of the island's northern half provide shelter in all but the severest conditions, and Eagle Hill to the south, whose verdant summit affords a stunning 360-degree view of the lough, has the kind of exposed, precipitous grazing favoured by sheep the world over. Assuming word gets around — and if the racket outside our bedroom window at first light on a spring morning is anything to go by, I'm certain it does — our woolly neighbours would surely give

Islandmore top slot in any *Which Pasture* poll for Variety of Single-file Walks, Difficulty of Footing, Flavour of Grass and Overall Quality of Short Life. Short, sadly, being the operative word. On a walk round the island foreshore one day we came upon James separating the ewes from that season's lambs, which he loaded onto the barge for market, and we learned that the only sound more wretched than a lamb in search of its mother is 150 more in search of theirs. We felt heart-sorry for both groups of bereft and bewildered animals. The ewes bunched up by the water as the barge pulled away, and it was several hours before bleats of outrage and loss yielded to the rumble of 150 empty stomachs, and heads began to go down one by one as they spread out over the hill in search of grass. Even for them life goes on and thank goodness, like us, they cannot know for how long.

The approach to the jetty, no matter that I have made it a thousand times, has a way of lifting my spirits and it must have done something for Jo, too, because he frightened the life out of me by stretching his arms wide and treating me, and the rest of the lough, to a rendition of 'Home, Home on Ze Range' at the top of his not inconsiderable lungs. When I very much didn't sing along, the delivery, from line two, became increasingly *sotto voce*, until by the end of the first verse I could barely make out that ze sky was not cloudy or grey. However, that's because I was just two feet from a boisterous outboard motor, whereas Lynn, working in her studio a good half-mile away on the far side of the cabin, was not; *alors – quel plaisir –* apparently she was able to enjoy the whole performance from, as it were, the front row.

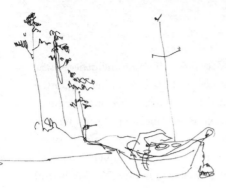

Twenty-two

Visitors, and preparations for visitors, provided a welcome distraction through late winter and spring from the creeping realisation that I was heading for personal bankruptcy. There was a steady trickle of orders for my fledgling bed company, but having used the sale proceeds from the house to repay my business borrowing and take care of trade creditors from the Edinburgh business, there was little left for investment in materials, marketing, or even getting to the workshop on a regular basis.

Through the winter months, on the promise of a six-week delivery for beds, I had been in the habit of waiting until there was more than one order and then booking a cheap return flight to Edinburgh on a two- or three-day turnaround. I would set the alarm for 4.30 a.m., stumble about lighting candles, pull on oilskins and row out for the With; grab a cup of tea, whisper goodbyes to Lynn and leave the island by five; put the With on the mooring at the yacht club and row in to the pontoons; take off the gear in the boat park, drive to Aldergrove, fly to Edinburgh, catch a bus as far as The Gyle and walk to the railway station; catch a train to Inverkeithing, change for Cowdenbeath and walk the last half-mile to the workshop, where I would arrive, ill-tempered and in pain, at around two in the afternoon – time enough to cut components and book a haulier for two days hence at ten in the morning to deliver boxed Santa Fe beds to Stornoway, or Knightsbridge, or Draycott in the Moors. By 9 p.m., after a fish supper from the top of the road, I would be asleep on the camp bed on the workshop floor, and for the next forty-eight hours it would be more of the same until I gratefully handed over a consignment note, said cheerio to the van driver and set off on the same rather disjointed journey in reverse, arriving back at the jetty in time for supper.

Every couple of weeks I went through the motions but the writing was on the wall: an order a week wasn't going to take the business anywhere and I wasn't in a position to pay for more advertising.

I took odd jobs between runs to Scotland, mainly for family and friends, but it was subsistence at best and no matter how many fences mysteriously required to be built, or rooms painted, my immediate family couldn't keep finding jobs to pay me for indefinitely. In a valiant effort to do just that, my mother would call me up, as she has done for years, with small computer problems and I would spend an hour or two sorting them out with her; but whereas in the past I had simply been the family computer expert, I seemed now to have achieved consultancy status, and of course consultants don't come cheap. We would periodically enter into a kind of reverse haggle, where she would say, 'Now, let me give you a cheque', and I would say, 'Don't be silly', and she would say, 'If I had to pay a professional, it would cost me a fortune!' Similar rituals were played out with David and Claire.

We may expect such kindnesses from family, but the most unexpected people can be extraordinarily generous. A year earlier, when I finally decided to call it a day and close the main business in Edinburgh, I began phoning my suppliers, some of whom went back fifteen years.

When I got to Ashoke Pasi, who runs a wholesale furniture business with his brother in Glasgow, he said: 'Mike, I don't mean to pry, but it all sounds a bit bleak.'

'It's been better,' I said.

'I'm not rich but I can give you a thousand pounds today if that would help. No need to give it back.'

Given that I already owed his company for goods supplied, it was an offer I couldn't possibly take up, but the gesture was worth a great deal more to me than a thousand pounds.

Another exhibit for my gallery of heroes.

I can admit to myself now that it was optimistic to rely for future income on the little bed business that remained. Through the winter our resources steadily dwindled and my bed-building trips to

Cowdenbeath became, if anything, a further drain while orders were so sporadic. The rump of personal debt we had carried forward became impossible to service and by April it was clear that the sale of the house, in terms of solvency, had been no more than a time-buying exercise, albeit an infinitely valuable one.

With feelings of *déjà vu*, I decided to wind down the bed business, and at the same time I took the plunge and instructed a Belfast firm to petition for my bankruptcy before someone else did. A hearing was fixed for a week and a half hence and while the days of public humiliation in open court are mercifully gone, private humiliation is still with us and I can think of better ways to spend a Monday afternoon.

Afterwards Lynn, as always, was more philosophical than I was, and more practical. Whereas I would say, 'Now what are we going to do?', she would say, 'Now. What are we going to do?' It was Lynn who suggested I top up my odd-job income and take advantage of my new-found spare time by doing some writing, something I had dabbled at back in Scotland. She was full of ideas – short stories, a column on island life, perchance a book – to which I was enthusiastically receptive, having had secret ambitions in that direction ever since the triumphant discovery that I had been the only one in class to complete a challenging poetry assignment during evening prep. I still have the original.

> I have to write a poem
> But I don't know what to write
> If I don't think of something
> I'll be here throughout the night.
>
> It only is a mater (*sic*)
> Of words inside a book
> Oh look I've written something
> But it's only just a fluke.

Faulkner II (aged 9)

Apparently some of the others had been staring at blank sheets of paper for forty-five minutes, or folding them into those rectangular aeroplanes with stand-up tail that fly in a circle if you make one wing flap bigger than the other.

While I have snuck in my masterpiece here, I realise it's not of publishable quality, but it does illustrate an early inkling of one of the most effective remedies – words, *any* words, on paper – for writer's block.

Having sorted me out, we turned our attention to Lynn. With such poor natural light, none of the little rooms at the back of the cabin was much good as a working studio, but she had made temporary use of one anyway to produce work for the galleries and for the various annual exhibitions in the Royal Scottish Academy in Edinburgh. The year before our move, she had been elected to the prestigious Royal Scottish Society of Painters in Watercolour, so it was not a good time to take a sabbatical from her work.

She urgently needed a studio with proper light, and we found one in the shape of a garden shed for which my brother no longer had any use. I calculated that at six by eight feet it was one-sixteenth the size of the studio at Quilchena, but it had adequate headroom, a heavy floor and plenty of glass on two walls. It duly arrived at the pontoons, dismantled and stacked on David's trailer, and we transferred it section by section onto the With, topping off with the steeply pitched felt roof, which was still in one piece. With three of us and the entire shed on board, deck space was at a premium for the crossing and Jock scrambled up the slope of the roof and inched his way forward to perch there, a proud and shaggy prow, scrabbling every so often to regain the apex of the roof as the whole unlikely ensemble swayed and wallowed its progress over the sound.

Lynn was so excited. She couldn't wait to put it together but,

typically, her mind was already on the detail, way ahead of me. While I was working out the foundations and the size of the deck, which I planned to build out over the water, she was making faces at the standard shed-orange finish and dabbing variants of the house colour onto bits of scrap timber. I was sufficiently infected by her excitement to get started immediately and I began driving posts into the ground as close to the water's edge as I dared, a little way from the cabin, nailing on a framework of old joists as I went.

When the foundation was ready, we dropped the floor into position and raised the gable end. Lynn braced herself against it from the outside and I lifted the first side wall so that it stood at right angles to the gable.

'Don't move,' I said.

I gripped part of the frame with one hand and reached for a hammer and a three-inch nail with the other; but I hadn't reckoned on the breeze coming off the water, and the wall was snatched out of my hand and dropped on its back in the grass.

With both arms stretched high and wide above her, and the side of her face flattened against the wall, Lynn couldn't see what was happening and she kept saying, 'Is that it? Have you got it? Can I let go, please?' and I kept saying 'No! Hold on, almost there', until after several tries I did get a nail into the corner, and we stood back to admire the beginnings of a proper working studio, albeit a very, very small one.

'It's very small, isn't it?' said Lynn.

'Think Dr Who,' I said.

By dark it was fully assembled, and the following day Lynn got to work with a paintbrush while I devised ways to maximise the space inside. I lined one wall with shelves exactly the depth of her paint pots, made her working table corner-shaped and put hinges on a second table and a stool so they could be dropped down when not in use. The 'piece of resistance', as my father used to say, was a two foot by two foot square of plywood on four locking wheels, designed to obviate the need for Lynn to come at her paintings from all sides while she worked them up on the floor: instead, in theory, they would now come to her.

It worked a treat. By mid-afternoon Lynn had had a successful dry run, using a blank board on the studio floor, and we sat cross-legged on her little bleached-wood deck with only a very nautical-looking fence made from a looping length of three-ply hemp rope between us and the water. She smiled and patted the boards with the flat of her hand, happy and no doubt relieved to be in a space of her own for the first time since leaving Quilchena. I knew that the psychological gap between the studio and the cabin would be a great deal wider than the physical one, allowing her once again to inhabit two worlds and feeding the fires of her benign artistic schizophrenia.

For my part, if things were coming together for Lynn, they were coming together for me.

Twenty-three

Now and again people who don't know us very well have said things like, 'Quite a change of lifestyle, isn't it?' They look at Lynn and we can see that the question is directed mainly at her and is code for 'How do you cope with the isolation?'

Our answer is to point towards the boat – two boats lashed together, in fact – moored close to the far side of Ringhaddy Sound. For twenty-three years Alan and Rae McGarvey have lived on the water – and before that they ran a Post Office in east Belfast. *That* is a change of lifestyle. *Sir Henry Morgan* is a cement-hulled schooner of 74 feet, a good-looking boat before her mast was unstepped and laid along her deck; and tied to her is *Eleanor Laura*, an ex-Belfast harbour launch, a little smaller and more workmanlike than handsome. Both have seen better days, and their decks are so encumbered with timber, buoys, engines and the omnium gatherum of a quarter century of family life that from a distance their profiles bleed together and it's hard to separate one from the other. However, as I have told a number of visitors on their first crossing of the sound, who look over and say, 'What is *that*?': if you don't have a back yard, or a garage, or a skip in the supermarket car park at the end of the road, you are inevitably going to gather, well, stuff. Besides, as I also tell them, the setup has character.

The McGarveys have two sons, to whom, of course, boats are second nature. When Connor went to sea, an early class during training was knots. Connor can tie a one-handed bowline behind his back, and shortly into the first lesson the instructor had an idea. 'OK,' he said. 'Two groups. Connor, you take the left …'

Tragically, the family would have been five. Rae was aboard one day with the two younger boys when she went below to answer the phone. The boys were playing on deck. Connor, who was just a toddler, came to the hatch and told his mother that Ali was 'swimming'. Rae was at the rail in seconds but there was nothing she could do. She couldn't swim and Allaistair was already under the water. The cruelty of her predicament is beyond imagining.

Allaistair was just four years old. That Alan and Rae continued to live on the boat afterwards is testament to their courage and their sense of commitment to the lifestyle. To leave the boat, they say, would have been to run away.

Had isolation been a problem for us, the McGarveys' high-speed comings and goings and the dim glow of their cabin lights might have been reassuring features of our island existence, as on long winter nights there is little other sign of life on the sound; but as we have actively sought isolation most of our adult lives, neither of us has felt the need for such signs of civilisation, or quasi-civilisation.

On the other hand, we did soon discover that in such practical matters as the weather, the safest places to leave the dinghy in the hours before a big wind, who owns what and lives where, and which moorings are vacant and therefore available to visitors, Alan McGarvey is the man. It was Alan, on a pleasant afternoon in April, who motored over to the jetty and suggested we might like to take the With off her mooring and tie her to the northeast side of the quay along the foreshore before turning in for the night. There, he explained, she would have good shelter however severe the gale, which would be coming from the west.

'West?' I said. 'Gale?' And then, back-pedalling in the direction of wisdom and foresight, 'You reckon it will be that bad?'

'Put it this way,' he said. He leaned forward a little and a light came on in his rather piercing blue eyes. I knew him well enough to recognise the precursors to a story, sometimes a long one. He looked at the stand of pines behind me and said: 'I was on the boat the day your trees came down.'

This was the same afternoon in February 1982 that my uncle took his famous photograph. John Scott has talked about it too and I have the impression it is one of those signally memorable days for which anyone living by the sea can call up their own personal store of images, graphic and indelible. For Uncle Dennis there is the dinghy in flight over Islandmore. For John Scott, standing on the floating pontoons, there is an ecliptic moment of brooding and expectant stillness and a distant rushing from the southeast before the wind comes headlong, like a herd on the stampede, over the Ringdufferin headland and into the sound. And for Alan there is another inflatable dinghy, horizontally suspended by its bow rope from the stern of *Connaught*, the late Conn McCann's ill-fated Galway hooker, quivering in the wind as though on davits, above a vaporous torrent of flying spray.

'Not,' said Alan, 'that I could afford to be a spectator.'

With his floating home pitching beneath his feet, and Rae below decks and pregnant, he was potentially separated from catastrophe by the weakest link, wherever that might be, in a series of shackles and chains running from a pair of mooring cleats on the forward deck, via the anchor winch to the mooring buoy on the surface of the sound, and finally to the sea bed, and his more than ample mooring: sixty feet of doubled inch-and-a-half steamer chain fed through the spokes of two railway wheels, a pair of Harland and Wolff lathe beds with a combined weight of more than a ton, and a huge fisherman's anchor.

With winds gusting to ninety miles an hour, he kept anchor watch all afternoon, going between saloon and deck to check the mooring, able to breathe only with his back to the wind, holding on to anything grabbable. He will have seen, heard, felt as much drama in those few hours as many of us will experience in a decade, but in the end his mooring held and by evening the storm had blown itself out and he was able to relax. Only then did he take the time to look around, and along with much else that had changed, most of the trees in the planting by the cabin were down. The building itself, favoured by the accident of wind direction, was untouched.

Generally speaking, in Ringhaddy terms, Alan has been there and done that. He is never stuck for an answer if you say, 'Any ideas?' and on several occasions I have said just that. When John Scott reported one afternoon that he had heard a whining or crying sound coming from under the pontoons and that despite putting an ear to the gaps, he couldn't quite work out where or what it was, I motored over to *Sir Henry Morgan* to enlist Alan's help in a rescue mission. Rescuing what, I had no idea. John was thinking a cat, which seemed plausible enough, and I was thinking up ways to take a look without drowning myself: I am not comfortable under the water at the best of times, but when there are chains, and steel beams, indeterminate depths, curtains of impenetrable seaweed and crazed kittens down there, I need all the moral support I can get. John having headed home for the day, I turned to Alan.

'Let's take a look,' he said, the glint of adventure in his eye. He shouted through the saloon hatch: 'Connor! Bring some gear, there's something under the pontoons! We're going to have a look.'

Connor appeared with a canvas holdall and two wet suits. He held one out towards me.

'This one do?' he said. 'It fits Andrew.'

'I ... yes,' I said. 'Thanks.'

Alan said: 'Leave your dinghy here, we'll take the dory.'

The three of us sped the quarter-mile back to the pontoons, and when we got there, Connor and I squeezed ourselves into the wet suits. Alan took on the role of director of operations, at which he excels, and from the holdall he produced helmet, goggles and snorkel and instructed me, against my better judgement, to put them on. Next out, flippers. I put those on too, and stood there like an idiot, Alan's gesticulating figure only half-seen through mercifully misted Perspex, his highly specific instructions coming as a muffled murmur through the rubber of my asphyxiatingly tight helmet. He walked over to the point at which John had last heard something, and motioned first Connor, then me, to stand on opposite sides of the pontoon. He pointed towards his feet and I heard him say 'air space', which didn't encourage me at all, if that's what it was meant to do. He rummaged again in the holdall and came out with a torch. Great idea, I thought, and grabbed it before he could offer it to Connor.

Then one last time he reached in the bag and came out with something flattish and about two feet long, which he indicated was for me. I didn't know what it was, so I wasn't keen and waited for clearer instructions. Alan was saying something and flexing the thing in his hands, and then he put it around his waist and I caught the word 'lead' and something like 'keep you down!' Understanding and horror came to me at the same time. I peered out at Alan from my hermetically sealed and increasingly claustrophobic world and thought: Are you out of your mind? The last accessory I needed at that moment was something designed to keep me down there longer.

I said: 'No. I'll be fine. Thanks though.'

Alan gave a big thumbs up and Connor and I sat on the edges of the pontoon with our backs to each other. I was getting my thoughts together and gathering up the courage to go in the water when I heard a splash behind me, which invoked sufficient competitive instinct to make me push myself off the edge. I went under momentarily and surfaced close enough to the pontoon to hold on for a few moments. Then I thought, Now or never, and duck-dived, swimming awkwardly down and at an angle I calculated would bring me up in the fabled air space whose existence I had so far had to take on faith.

When I thought I'd gone far enough, I turned over and thrashed my flippered feet about in a way which I hoped would propel me in the direction of the sky. The first thing I encountered was something hard and unyielding. I realised that I was stuck by my own flotation to the underside of the concrete walkway, and having no idea what way I was facing, I began to panic. I clawed my way forwards until my fingers found an edge, and pulled as hard as I could, popping up like a cork beside Connor, having 'swum' the full width of the pontoon.

When I got my breath back, I said to Connor, with under-statement: 'I didn't see very much, did you?' To which he replied: 'All I can say is that it's big and furry. I couldn't really see without the torch.' Clearly we had both been busy but in different ways.

So down we went again, and this time, to my indescribable relief, I came up in exactly the right spot. Each pontoon floats on three massive blocks of polystyrene, separated from one another by little more than a head's width of air; and above these blocks, immediately under the walkway, is another air space that is even bigger. I pulled myself up far enough to hook my free arm over the top of the float, and swept the torch from side to side in front of me.

The first thing I saw, directly across, was Connor's head. He said, 'Try over there', and pointed into the corner. In that confined space, surrounded by water and steel and presumably with acoustical help from the polystyrene, I was able to hear every word. I followed his pointing finger and the beam came to rest, not on the green eyes of a stray tabby but the black button eyes of a clearly startled, but just as clearly unintimidated, otter. It stared into the light and I could see every whisker of its very beautiful face, and the pale splash of its chest. It was backed tightly into the corner, arched and tense, its long tapering tail lying along the edge where the float met the steel casing. For a few moments none of the three of us moved a muscle or made a sound, and those few moments I have carefully filed away in a special catalogue of memories, heading Experiences, sub-heading Sublime.

Far from being rescuers, we were clearly intruders. I knew from local lore that otters had occasionally been seen in the area over the years, but not for a long time – certainly, no one was aware that they had taken up residence. But why wouldn't they? A big warm chunk of polystyrene with a concave top surface, roofed over with concrete, would seem to be the perfect place to raise a family.

We left him – or her – to it and retreated. I made a pretty good fist of returning to the surface, and I didn't say as much to Connor or his father but I have a fair idea which of us – me or the otter – had had the scariest experience that afternoon.

Scary or not, though, it doesn't compare with poor Jock's earlier experience at almost exactly the same spot. Lynn and I had been off the island for the day. We arrived back at the boat park after midnight, and as usual I left Lynn to organise the dogs and off-load the gear from the car while I went to fetch the With from the mooring. Jock came with me, which was a bit unusual – normally he would wait for Lynn – and he was standing on the pontoons when I rowed away.

For some reason the With's outboard had been playing up and I pulled the start cord a dozen times without success. I tried the choke full in, full out and in every position between. My arm aching, I sat on the stern locker and waited.

Meantime Lynn had arrived at the pontoons. Not being greeted by Jock, she assumed I had taken him with me in the rowing boat. She couldn't see me in the darkness but she heard me trying to start the motor, and knew I would be waiting to give it another go.

Standing there in the quiet, she heard an odd sound – a low, persistent wheezing – coming from somewhere below her feet. She knelt on the edge and peered into the water. At the point where two pontoons meet there is a single chain link that lies just below the surface, and Jock had managed to rest his chin there. Only his little snout was visible, and whatever frantic efforts he had already made to get himself onto the pontoon, by the time Lynn found him he was barely moving. His throat constricted by the weight of his own body as he hung precariously from the pontoon, he was forced to take in air through clenched teeth; and at that point, had Lynn been unable to find him, his life might easily have been measured in seconds.

Lynn scooped him out of the water and held him in her arms, and then she began to think about just how close the call had been, and slipped into something like a state of shock. When I made it back to the pontoons, having finally got the outboard started, I found her sitting on the concrete with Jock on her lap, sobbing. She kept saying, 'Poor Jock; oh poor Jock' over and over, and even Rab was visibly affected, standing quietly and uncertainly off to the side.

I bundled the three of them into the boat, and back on the island we wrapped Jock in blankets and put him in front of the stove, where he promptly fell into a deep, unstirring sleep, moving not an inch until next morning.

For Lynn, it was the traditional remedy of hot tea and Marmite on toast while we conducted a postmortem. A little unsteady in the dark at the best of times, Jock must simply have stepped backwards or sideways off the pontoon, and we shuddered to think what would have happened if there had been no ledge on which to rest his head; or indeed, if the outboard had started first time. In one eventuality he wouldn't have made that curious sound; and in the other, we wouldn't have heard him even if he had.

Twenty-four

Sadly for the otters, a few weeks after our diving adventure, work began on a much-heralded and rather controversial project to upgrade the facilities at the yacht club. Controversial, because the idea was to replace the floating pontoons, many of which bottomed out with every tide and had begun to show their age, with a fixed horizontal walkway on concrete piers running from the high-water line to just above low-water and joined by a swinging bridge to a brand new 'floating harbour' of pontoons occupying the same footprint as the old: a costly and aesthetically doubtful operation that split the club membership into irreconcilable camps. Those against on cost grounds were joined by others who foresaw, with uncanny prescience, the amenity impact of something in the style of a motorway flyover jutting out into the sound.

As yet merely temporary club members, Lynn and I were entitled to attend the highly charged extraordinary general meetings that preceded the final decision but not, unfortunately, to vote. In the end, those in favour won in the teeth of a large and vociferous minority, who, with an eye to the beauty of the area or the contents of their wallets, or both, fought fiercely for the more conservative and rather cheaper option of like for like.

The otters would be the greater losers, their cosy polystyrene bolt holes gone for good. We worried about them at first, and then one morning in late summer, many weeks after work was completed, Lynn's eye was taken by a movement at the far end of the jetty as she came out of her studio. Oblivious to her presence, an otter was enjoying a picnic in the sunshine. One front paw was firmly planted on his still flapping victim and he was tearing off silvery strips with his teeth. Rab, whose nose, eyes and sense of the unfamiliar are as keen as they ever were, stood rigid and staring on the little deck in front of the studio. Lynn lifted a finger and whispered pre-emptively, 'No! Shshh!', but to no avail. A low growl rose in the back of Rab's throat and emerged from his mouth in the form of an experimental and slightly uncertain bark, a warming up exercise for whatever call to arms might shortly be expected of him; and at that, with hardly a splash, the otter was off the jetty and gone, leaving his meal behind. It turned out to be a good-sized dogfish, a species quite common in Strangford Lough whose other, more romantic, name of rock salmon belies its membership of the order *Selachii*, or shark.

Anyway, for better or worse, the bridge to nowhere was duly built. It gleams in the morning sun, a permanent hard-edged feature of its softer surroundings, thrusting proudly eastwards over the sound. At low-water it stands twelve feet above the shingle, trouncing its predecessor by a margin of nine feet and six inches, towering over its attendant mini-harbour of pontoons configured as an enormous floating capital E. They built me because they could, it seems to say.

Even after dark it makes its presence felt. There has been a change in the night-time view from the island, a less than subtle reminder that even out of the waters of this hitherto unspoilt corner of the lough, technology manages to rear its ugly head.

Before, with nightfall there always came a rich and enveloping blanket in shades of grey, a finely rendered and ever-changing grisaille by the hand of Nature herself. The hand of Man, from the cabin at any rate, could be seen only in the lights of three or four houses half-hidden in the drumlined folds of the mainland opposite, or the handful of moored boats lying in black silhouette against the water. Otherwise, there was just the intervening stretch of sea, never quite dark even on moonless nights but with a dull reflective gleam; the low black undulations of a skyline spiked by little stands of larch and pine against the distant city glow; and, above, the graduated charcoal blue immensity of the night sky.

Looking to the north, even if I couldn't see them, I could always mark the floating pontoons in my mind from the run of the skyline and the disposition of the house lights. Heading that way by boat, as we approached out of the darkness the pontoons would take form by degrees. Each trip, in fact, was something of an adventure; but once close in, the margin of safety was determined not by chance but by common sense and an awareness, quickly acquired by anyone who uses boats, that on the water in darkness it is not the straight-on but the peripheral vision that picks up mooring buoys, small boats and other potential hazards.

Late one night, by way of illustration, I had just shut down the generator and was climbing the steps to the veranda, holding a torch in front of me, when I met Lynn's mother in dressing gown and slippers. She was leaning on the rail, gazing out over the water.

Sounding a little perplexed, she said: 'Mike?'

'Marion.'

'I don't know what it is but every time I look at the dinghy it disappears.'

It's quite true and the trick, when you're on the water, is to scan to left and right more or less continuously and to build up a mental picture by which a path (fog excepted) can be threaded between any number of obstacles that would otherwise be near-invisible. Stare hard at individual objects – wish them into place – and they have an uncanny, not to say disconcerting, habit of disappearing.

Now, though, it's as if someone has taken the magic away. The most striking feature of the nocturnal landscape is a flashing red light; put there, I suspect, with the engineering equivalent of a final flourish, *la touche finale*, as part of the installation of the new pontoons. It blinks insistently on a five-second relay from dusk till dawn, without, as far as I can gather, serving much useful purpose. No one claims that the bottom of the sound is littered with the rusting hulks of numberless boats fated on stormy nights to strike the pontoons and go down with all hands; not, at any rate, for want of a flashing light. This isn't Cape Terror but one of the most sheltered and congenial natural anchorages in the lough. Someone must have been carried away. 'A flashing light! Can we have a flashing red light? Oh *please* say we might!'

It's not just island-dwellers like us who can't escape. Curiously, in what must feel to the two houses adjacent to the pontoons like a kind of Chinese torture, the light is designed to be seen through 360 degrees, which means that even as you drive into the boat park from the road, there it is, blinking away from the far end of the pontoons –

the night-time equivalent of a sign saying, Water: Proceed by Boat.

We have become used to it, as you do. I've even found some romance in it. I think of Jay Gatsby, for whom the green light at the end of some distant jetty came to symbolise his beloved Daisy, and I feel better about it.

Which is more than I can say for the card-operated electronic steel barrier that was installed at the entrance to the cruising club's car park as part of the same project. An eight-foot-high grille made from galvanised box section, which would, if it weren't for the thorn hedges and green fields, the rocky foreshore and the loveliness of the sound, blend sympathetically with its surroundings, it beeps obsequiously when offered a white plastic key card and slides open, bowing and scraping, to admit Members Only. Riffraff – retired couples walking the dog, nature lovers or just lovers – now have to look elsewhere to find access to the prettier parts of the lough, something which has become increasingly difficult.

The barrier was put up to discourage theft of outboard motors and other equipment from the boat park and there is, in fairness, a history of things going missing – I lost some gear myself during the winter. On the other hand, when I lived in a quiet area of old Edinburgh, my car was broken into three times in as many years, and it wasn't in the option of the residents' committee to erect security barriers at each end of the street.

I wonder what Gatsby would have made of it. Perhaps he would see the barrier not in terms of social exclusion and élitism but – another of Fitzgerald's themes – of changing times, nostalgia and philosophical acceptance. Perhaps we should go with the flow and count ourselves lucky that along with the McGarveys, who have been twenty-three years on their boat, we live in a gated community of two.

Castle Ward

Twenty-five

As if to put small gripes in perspective, the first tern arrived in the same week as the construction equipment. I was struggling down from the yacht club car park with a gas canister on my shoulder and as many carrier bags as I could grip with my free hand, when I spotted its long white tail feathers poking out from among the coils of the lifebuoy rope on the very outside edge of the last pontoon. It didn't bother to rise even when I dropped my stuff into the With with a clatter and started the motor, so I stepped onto the pontoon again and walked very slowly to within ten or twelve feet, close enough to look down and take in the pale grey wing feathers tucked back and crossed over the porcelain white, and surprisingly tiny, body; and the black-capped head, beady black eyes and telltale black tip of its red-orange beak – the only way I know to tell a common tern from an Arctic tern. Even then, it remained motionless and it was still there when I pulled away.

Little wonder: it had come a long way. These beautiful birds, the 'swallows of the sea', come to breed on Strangford Lough but they can spend the winter as far south as the Antarctic; and during the first half of April, after a record-breaking round trip of up to ten thousand miles, they begin to arrive in a steady trickle of exhausted individuals, settling on the boats and mooring buoys in the sound for a day or two before heading off in search of food and a mate.

Endearingly schizophrenic, when terns are on the hunt they bounce and hover and dance in the air like butterflies as they scour the water for fish, their heads tipped downwards the better to bring their most powerful weapon – their amazing eyesight – to bear, and occasionally diving with deadly accuracy from thirty or forty feet above the waves. But when there are young nearby the same dainty and earnest birds become psychopathically protective and their furious, shrieking dives are directed not at little fish but at anything that moves. They can draw blood from a person's head, and only the very adventurous – not to say disrespectful – bird-watcher will venture among the breeding colonies in May or June.

Of these colonies, one of the busiest is Dunnyneil Island, and on one of our many trips to Portaferry we landed on the larger of its two uneven mounds, as far as we could get from the biggest concentration of nesting gulls, and had a conscience-plagued picnic, during which an indignant population of terns and black-headed gulls rose from their nests and hurled abuse, as it seemed to us, from the sky above the little mound at the other end of the island. When it was clear we were neither going away nor coming any closer, they settled into an uneasy acceptance and landed again, and as they did so we watched through binoculars as the ground between them came to life with a scurrying army of mottled brown, perfectly camouflaged young who were off the nests but unable, as yet, to fly. Hitherto invisible, they must have been told in no uncertain terms to lie doggo, not to move a muscle, and the earlier shrieks had obviously been directed not just at us, but at them: as much 'Stay where you are!' as 'Get out of here!'

This time, our guest was Lynn's oldest friend, Jessica 'Puddleduck'

Bevan, another graduate of the art college in Edinburgh and another
sickeningly talented artist. Her speciality is botanically correct,
exquisitely rendered watercolours of flowers, but with a twist: in one
piece, her sea holly has as a background a faded abstraction of the cross
of Saint Andrew, and in another, two stalks of Cape gooseberries are
placed with sure compositional skill amongst an arrangement of crazed
gold-leaf panels, which are irreversibly applied with impressive
courage after the flowers have been painted – a process that may itself
have taken weeks.

Jessica's nickname comes from my innocent mistake, on first
meeting her many years ago, of thinking her name was Jemima; but
others have always assumed that it has something to do with her
unquestionably noble profile – a family trait – and that assumption, at
least between the three of us, has grown wings over the years, so that
these days it is hard to have even a simple exchange of text messages
without throwing in a couple of puerile duck jokes:

'Fly into Belf 10.30 am. Quack visit. Pud.'

'Why nt fly into R/haddy? Watch out 4 wildfowlers, heard shots
this am.'

At least, as often as not, she starts it.

Anyway, Puddleduck became our most frequent visitor from
Scotland and she was with us on Dunnyneil. After a sandwich picnic,
I left her catching up with Lynn, grabbed my camera and climbed
carefully upwards and into the tangle of briars and long grass that
fringed the hillock behind us: carefully, because I was looking for
something particular, of which I used to find many as a teenager. I had
hardly started when one appeared directly in front of me, or rather,
materialised, because that's the extraordinary effect of a mallard on the
nest: you tend to see first an eye, as it catches the light, and then the
rest of the brown body by degrees as its uncannily blended outline
disentangles itself from the leaves and dried grass around it.

I took a digital photograph of my unblinking subject and turned
back to see what the others were up to. I could hear peals of laughter
coming from the beach, and not for the first time I was thankful,
primarily on Lynn's behalf, for close friends. She had, of course, fallen
comfortably enough into island life because she is such a can-do and
self-reliant person, but more than at any time in her life, the continuity
provided by contact with friends from Scotland had taken on great

significance. The inevitable question, 'How long do you think you'll be on the island?' always produced the inevitable reply: 'Until we can afford to return to Scotland'; and eventually, I could see, we could well be looking for a place on the west coast or in the northeast of Scotland. Not the central belt: that would be too painful. John and Emma Hawkins had asked us several times to visit, not to mention Sam, but we hadn't yet summoned the courage to do so; it would mean turning into our old lane and then forking off to their barn conversion. Sooner or later we would, as Lynn would say – nobody mixes metaphors like Lynn – bite the bull by the horns and go back, but it would be with eyes averted: Quilchena would be there, dead ahead, and the fifty yards of lane to John and Emma's right fork would be a long, long way.

I found the girls where I'd left them.

'Wait till you see this, Puddleduck,' I said. I had been to a place of magic and wonder, but without the evidence I wasn't sure my earth friends would believe me. I pressed the camera's review button and held up the little screen for Jessica to see. 'What do you think?'

'Of what?' she said, squinting.

'What do you mean? You of all people.'

I turned the camera round to have a look myself.

'It's ...' I began. But sure enough, all I could see was a patch of rough grass and some twigs.

'... a duck,' I said. So perfect was the bird's camouflage that no matter what way I turned the screen, I couldn't persuade her to show herself.

A place of magic and wonder, I repeated to myself, and left it at that. (Later, on the computer, I blew the picture up to full screen and there she was in all her inscrutable glory. Jessica nodded gravely and said: 'Kin.')

I'm afraid we managed to set the gulls on edge again as we left Dunnyneil and turned towards Portaferry, but they settled quickly once we were on the water.

It's one of the features of Strangford Lough, looking to the south, that at first glance it appears land-locked: the Narrows channel is somewhat offset, forming an elbow where it joins the lough and running from northwest to southeast for two miles to the sea, so that the effect as you approach from the north is of a continuous run of land, higher, craggier and with many more trees than elsewhere, but lacking an obvious exit. It means that as the boat begins to kick and swerve in the cross-currents at the approach to the Narrows, and the steeply wooded channel finally begins to reveal itself, the beauty of this part of the lough comes as a succession of delightful surprises.

The first is a deep and sheltered bay cut into the west shore in an area known as Audley's Roads. In contrast to the fertile slopes further north, the shoulders of the bay rise as solid rock walls from the channel, topped with beech plantations spreading upwards and inwards to encircle a natural, sea-facing amphitheatre of open ground whose most prominent feature is Audley's Castle, a turreted, square-sided, fifteenth-century tower house with its own stone quay, a strategically perfect view of the lough and an air of timeless authority:

> I am monarch of all I survey,
> My right there is none to dispute.
> From the centre all round to the sea
> I am lord of the fowl and the brute.

We brought young Sam Hawkins here to look in on one of his screen favourites, the villain in *Shrek*, and as we climbed the switchback footpath from the quay his eyes became wider and his tongue more tied until he found himself standing in silent awe in front of the steel-studded oak door. Above, the castle walls receded to a vanishing point somewhere in the clouds and I don't know about Sam but I think I saw a raven circling the battlements and a silken kerchief flashing briefly white from a high window.

Lynn brought down her fist three times on the door and I brought my deepest and most stentorian voice to bear.

'Sam Hawkins for Lord Farquaad,' I announced. 'Sam Hawkins for Lord Farquaad!'

Sammy looked doubtful and took a backward step, his smile still intact but somehow more fixed. He was minded to stay put and skedaddle at the same time, so I made the decision for him.

'Here he comes. Run for it!' I said, and led the way down the hill at full tilt, Sam and Lynn at my heels in full voice: three small children with an age gap of forty years.

Halfway down we met Sam's parents coming up with the picnic, and we turned around. We ate in a walled enclosure at the foot of the castle, looking down on the anchorage: a few colourful sailing boats; the With tied up to an enormous steel ring on the side of the quay; across the Narrows to the southeast, the cluster of white buildings which is Portaferry; and half a mile to our right, high above the furthest point of the bay and half-hidden in the trees, Castle Ward House, erstwhile home of the Bangor family and now in the care of the National Trust. The first Baron Bangor and his wife, Lady Anne, who oversaw building operations in 1760, clearly had strong and sometimes incompatible views on things, because the east façade is gothic, in her taste, whereas the west is rigorously classical; and all the interior spaces are similarly and eccentrically juxtaposed.

Eccentricity must have run in the family because the sixth viscount, a keen sailor, made history in 1950 by becoming the object of Strangford Lough's first and only burial at sea. He insisted on it, and somewhere near the watery base of Angus Rock, at the entrance to the lough, lies his lead-lined coffin – or at least the lead lining of his coffin. The operation wasn't without hitches. His boatman didn't like the whole idea and is reputed to have said, 'On the third day the Lord will rise again'; the coffin was indeed washed ashore and had to be re-buried.

Several times we have been joined by schools of porpoises in the area outside the mouth of the bay at Audley's Roads, to varying degrees of delight or alarm from our guests. It was old hat to Lynn's mother, who often sees porpoises and dolphins in the Firth of Forth off Pittenweem. To the Hawkins boys it was a wondrous thing, a kind of open-skies Sea World performance exclusively for them. And to our friends Nigel and Joyce, for whose benefit the entire troupe of rolling, diving and dashing acrobats decided to head straight for the dinghy and then to roll and dive and dash underneath, it was, at least for Joyce, a bit like Sam and Lord Farquaad but without the option of flight. Fascinated by the bronze and silver flashes as they passed below us, she nevertheless glanced in my direction a couple of times and I had the impression that she was mentally weighing their size against the size of the boat.

Crossing the Narrows from Audley's Roads to Portaferry can be a nerve-jangling experience; not because the tidal run is at its swiftest there but because twice an hour, at o'clock and half-past, the car ferry pokes its head out from behind the harbour wall at Strangford village and prepares to make a bid for Portaferry. It strolls out into the relative calm close to shore with an air of relaxed and insouciant poise and then suddenly launches itself on a devil-may-care sprint into mid-channel, pitching itself on an easterly course across a current that acknowledges only north and south, and forcing smaller craft to play guessing games as to where it's likely to be relative to them in, say, seven seconds. Less experienced sailors – like me – abandon the helm and leave themselves at the mercy of the current until the blue-and-white monster has passed them by.

It's all over in six minutes. As the ferry eases in towards the landing ramp some of us are left wondering what almost hit us, but it's unwise to spend too long in contemplation because in another seven minutes it will be back for the return journey, following a similar but ever so slightly different zigzag course in reverse, just to keep us on our toes.

Twenty-six

Portaferry is a pleasant place to wander about but first, if you arrive by sea, you have to gain entry.

Like Ringhaddy, the marina suffers from steel-gate syndrome, but at least the key is a four-digit code rather than a plastic card and there is a helpful sign with the harbour master's phone number printed on it, so that visitors can get hold of the all-important access code for when they want to re-enter the marina. Arriving with Simon and Namaste, who live in the remote village of Ardfern on the west coast of Scotland, where a marina ten times the size is still protected by the more traditional devices of honesty and trust, we tied up the boat, buzzed ourselves out and made a note of the phone number for later.

Our guests were on the lookout for gifts to take home, so we called at the candle shop, where they sell little boxes in the shape of Irish cottages, containing Oxo-sized blocks of compressed turf, which smoulder to produce the authentic smell of the land of bogs and mists. Nothing, as they say, is added and nothing is taken away and they carry me instantly back to Mr Toner's 'caravan site', an otherwise empty field between the mountains and the sea at Roundstone in Connemara, where we three children raced boats made from leaves and twigs in a stream that widened into a dozen sandy fingers of clear mountain water where it emptied onto a Sahara-sized beach, and the all-permeating, never-forgotten scent of burning turf hung permanently in the air.

The other thing about Castle Hill Candles is that it is co-owned by a woman from West Texas, which tickles me.

To test Simon's contention that Guinness on the other side of the Irish Sea is a pale shadow of the stuff they serve in Irish pubs, we popped into Fiddler's Green further up the town. I was hoping for some live music because on an earlier mid-afternoon visit with John Hawkins and little Tom (Lynn and Emma had taken Sam to the excellent aquarium but we felt that while Tom was a little young for the aquarium, he had everything to gain from a visit to the pub) we were treated to an impromptu rendition, I think by the landlord himself, of 'The Secondhand Trousers I Bought in Belcoo', to the tune of 'Six Miles from Bangor to Donaghadee', during which Tom at first gaped incredulously at his host and then fell asleep. No luck with live music this time but the Guinness was apparently excellent and the atmosphere, as always, was warm and welcoming.

These days, broad-brush attributions of political persuasion to whole communities are hopefully becoming anachronistic, but traditionally Portaferry would have been of a nationalist stripe. My mother has vivid memories of an election meeting hosted by the East Down Unionist Association and addressed by my father, when the heckling became so threatening and sustained that the meeting had to be abandoned altogether. My parents retreated, with the usual police escort, to the ferry terminal, but the crowd which followed them seemed to have their own ideas as to how to fill the fifteen-minute wait before the ferry arrived, and when stones began bouncing off the car, Bill Connolly could stand it no longer and overruled my father. 'Never mind the bloody ferry!' he said, and led off at high speed on the fifty-mile detour up the Ards peninsula, across the top end of Strangford Lough and down the other side.

The political temperature has long since cooled. On yet another of our visits to Fiddler's, we had with us Lynn's sister, Fiona, and her husband, Geoff, who is a naval pilot. As with many men in the services, you can tell. The place was humming pleasantly and three or four locals whom I recognised as regulars were perched in a smoky row on stools at the bar. There were two girls serving and they obviously knew each other well because they kept up a happy banter while they took orders.

One of them turned to Fiona and said, 'What can I get you?'

Fiona looked along the line of bottles at the back of the bar, and at Geoff standing beside her, and said: 'A Black and Tan.'

It doesn't say much for me that I wondered if there might be any reaction. But it was obvious from her blank and innocent expression and her clearly Scottish accent that Fiona's cultural education could not be expected to include the story of the hated Black and Tans and the excesses they visited on nationalists in Ireland eighty years earlier, and that she was utterly unaware she might have been thought cheeky. Aside from one or two glances and the very briefest moment of silence, she wasn't. It's a welcome sign of the times that my paranoia was wholly misplaced.

I was telling Simon and Namaste the story of the Black and Tans as we walked back to the boat, and forgot to phone the harbour master for the access code. When we reached the gate, I dialled the telephone number and got a lady whom I took to be the harbour master's mother.

She said, 'You'll need to speak to Big John. Stay near the pontoons. I'll tell him you're waiting.'

'How will I know him?' I asked.

'You can't miss him. He'll tower above you.'

To pass the time, we wandered across the road to the coastguard station, where a 24-foot orange RIB is kept always at the ready for sea rescues, and chatted with a couple of lifeboatmen recently back from a training exercise.

I asked how often they were called out.

'In midsummer, when there are plenty of boats about, maybe two or three times a week,' one of them said.

Rather crassly I asked: 'Any life or death situations?'

'Not too often. But then' – he looked at his colleague – 'you never know how things might have gone if we hadn't turned up. And somebody has to do it.'

He told me they posted a log on their website, and although I was dying to press him for some details, I took a note of the address and said I would have a look when I got home.

A man in an oilskin jacket was walking towards us, but I didn't think it could be Big John because he wasn't especially big. *Tower above you*, his mother had said. However, as he approached he took a sheaf of receipts from his pocket, and said: 'I'll put the code on the back of the receipt.'

I stood beside him, guestimating our relative heights.

'You must be Bi ... you must be John.'

'How are you doing?' he said.

I had a feeling the visitor's fee had gone up from five pounds, but I said: 'There's a fiver. Don't worry about a receipt.'

He laughed. 'Ah now!' he said. 'Seven pounds.'

All of a sudden I understood what his mother had been talking about. I handed him another two pounds and said thanks, and as we walked away I said to Lynn: 'She meant "big" in an ethical, *incorruptible* way.'

'Tower above you morally,' said Lynn.

I did look up the coastguard website when we got home, and its service reports make delightful reading, as much for their tantalising omissions, their brevity and the measured, professional tone, as for actual tales of derring-do. Of incidents from the recent past, this was my favourite:

> 12–13 July 2000
> Yacht anchored in Knockinelder Bay, believed in danger of going aground. Portaferry Coastguard unable to attract attention of those on board after using searchlight, loud hailer and parachute flares. Portaferry Lifeboat launched 0010 13th July. On arrival at 0030, occupants awakened by lifeboat crew and yacht escorted to a safe anchorage in the area.

Wonderful. I couldn't help wondering what state these yachtsmen must have been in, and whether the date, the Twelfth of July, might offer a clue. *Unable to attract attention.* How could anyone sleep through searchlights, loud hailers *and* parachute flares? First a zillion candlepower is beamed through the portholes; then a coastguard officer uses a loud hailer to shout 'WAKE UP FOR GOODNESS SAKE!' at 150 decibels; and finally flares bright enough to light the Ards peninsula begin raining down onto the deck. None of this does the job. The spectacularly understated footnote – *On arrival at 0030, occupants awakened by lifeboat crew* – gives no clue as to how they were eventually roused, and I fondly imagine all six lifeboatmen tumbling through the hatch together, jumping up and down on the bunks and yelling 'Get up! Get up! You're all going to die!' at the top of their voices.

As they rightly say themselves, somebody has to do it.

Twenty-seven

From the beginning of May, after a long winter sleep, Ringhaddy Sound began to stir. In the space of a few weeks, as the boat park came alive and owners fussed happily around making last-minute preparations for the sailing season, we came to the hard realisation that for a few months at least, the sound would no longer be ours.

Oddly, I felt quite resentful. There is no more pleasant community than the community of sailors, but I had grown accustomed to early morning crossings in the company only of cormorants; to a final wave towards the cabin, in case Lynn was watching through binoculars, as I walked the length of a deserted pontoon in the half-light; and to the sound of the wind in the rigging of all those yachts clustered together on their trailers. Now the same yachts would go into the water in a more or less daily procession to the tune of the tides, courtesy of John Scott: at low water he would inch the trailers down the slipway behind his tractor, two to the tide, and deposit them there. In due course, with flotation, they would ease themselves astern and another happy yachtsman would motor off to pick up his mooring; all waves, bonhomie and high expectations.

It made up for the initial mild sense of invasion. High spirits being highly infectious, Lynn and I found that passing through the boat park as we left the island was like passing through the arrivals lounge at some exotic holiday destination: the atmosphere was full of promise and shared purpose, and everyone had time for everyone else.

Consequently, I had only to mention casually to Grahame Stronge that I thought the cabin's water supply might be leaking somewhere

under the sound, and he dropped everything.

Grahame so lives up to his name. Strong of arm, big of heart, he is the proverbial gentle giant. His boat, a fast 55-foot motor cruiser called *Sarah May III*, is one of a handful left in the water the year round to take advantage of those bright, crisp winter weekends with which Strangford is so generously endowed. I don't know why more people don't do it. Statistically, the lough is one of the driest pockets of Ireland, lying just outside the rain shadow of the Mourne Mountains. The seaside resort of Newcastle, twelve miles to the southwest, is positively rain-drenched by comparison.

Obviously, the down side of leaving your boat in the water is that you have to take the rough with the smooth, and when I mentioned our water problem, I think that Grahame, from personal experience of those days that are neither crisp nor bright, had instant empathy with us island-dwellers, for whom fair-weather boating is not an option. He probably imagined the horror of arriving on the island late at night and soaking wet, without the prospect of a bath; of washing from the jetty, flushing the toilet with buckets of seawater and carting drinking water across the sound in plastic drums, because he said with obvious concern, 'You don't really want to be on the island without water, do you?'

I knew that Grahame was a qualified diver, so there may have been an ulterior flavour to my reply.

'Not really,' I said. 'I think it's time for me to go swimming.'

'I could dive for the pipe and have a look,' he said.

Knowing about these things, he explained that freshwater, being significantly less dense than seawater, shows up as a gently ascending shimmer, which is fairly obvious in clear conditions; but we agreed that in the dark and muddy water of the sound he could spend for ever tracing the line of the alcathene pipe and still go past the break without seeing it.

In any case Grahame had another, more cunning plan.

'What about compressed air?' he said.

At first I didn't have an idea what he had in mind.

'Good idea,' I said. 'What do you have in mind?'

'One of my air bottles will deliver second stage pressure of 100 psi,' he said.

I nodded wisely.

'If we can isolate the pipe where it goes under the sound, and get an air line on it, we should be able to stay on the surface and look for the bubbles.'

It was an inspired idea, and as for isolating the pipe, there was a stop valve on the mainland beside the stone quay, and another on Islandmore just above the foreshore.

'How do we actually get air into the pipe?' I said.

'We need to make up a reducer to connect to the air bottle. What size is it?'

I knew the answer to that from conversations with James McFerran, who had laid the pipe himself more than forty years before, in order to bring drinking water to his stock on the island.

'Old three-quarter-inch,' I said.

'OK. We need to step down from three-quarter-inch alcathene to fifteen-mil brass. That will give them something to think about.'

He meant the plumber's merchant and he was right. An hour later I was standing at the counter of Jackie Brown's country hardware store, which tends to carry everything, including now-obsolete imperial pipe fittings.

I was relieved to see it was Jackie's son, Peter, behind the counter, because Jackie himself can be quite scary. I once wandered round the back of the counter and lost myself for some minutes amongst the racks of tools and ropes and farm supplies, utterly absorbed, and he frightened the life out of me by shouting, 'What are you doing back there?' from somewhere behind me. Bloomin' heck, won't do that again.

Peter said, 'What can I do for you?'

'I need to go, please, from this' – I drew a diagram – 'to this.'

Peter took the piece of paper and disappeared into the gloom of the same maze of racking. Every so often he popped out and stood under a fluorescent light holding together two bits of plastic, or a bit of plastic and a brass coupling, or a hose clip and a length of copper tube. He chatted away to himself at high speed.

'What about that, what's that, that's not it. Two of these and that there. No this here. That's you.'

He clattered half a dozen fittings and a roll of plumber's tape onto the counter and began to assemble them. Then he took a pencil from behind his ear and used the piece of paper with the diagram to total up the prices.

'Nine twenty-five. Nine pounds. Thank you, you're a gentleman.'

'Thank *you*,' I said. He knew his stuff.

I phoned Grahame from the car and we arranged to meet at the pontoons. On the way, I stopped off at the old quay and turned off the water supply at the meter.

Grahame's son, Mark, was with him, and we took their inflatable to Islandmore. We disconnected the pipe at the stop valve and used Peter's reducer, with which I could see Grahame was privately impressed, to connect up an air bottle. With everything in place, Mark stayed ashore with instructions to increase the pressure slowly on his father's signals, and Grahame and I took the inflatable out to the middle of the sound and cut the outboard.

We stood up, the better to see the surface of the water, and Grahame looked over at Mark and pointed upwards with one finger.

Conditions were perfect, with hardly a ripple, and we searched for a telltale line of bubbles. Nothing. Grahame jabbed his finger skywards with a little more urgency, and Mark gave a thumbs up and turned back to the regulator.

This time, the water erupted like a giant jacuzzi just feet away from the dinghy. It foamed and churned, and Grahame pointed frantically downwards and shouted for Mark to shut off the air.

'I think we can assume that's your leak!' he said.

We collected Mark and spent half an hour making passes to and fro in the general area of the leak, dragging a grappling hook behind us. When it eventually caught and held, we pulled it up hand over hand until we had a six-foot length of pipe draped over the bow of the dinghy.

I should say, Grahame pulled it up hand over hand. I tried, but as I struggled, more and more water-filled, barnacle-encrusted pipe left the sea bed and by the time it was halfway to the surface the effort was too much. I sweated and panted and held on, but I could raise it not one inch more, so I was pleased when Grahame said, 'Let me have a go.'

Grahame has been known to lift a forty-five-gallon drum of diesel onto the back of a trailer single-handed. He grabbed the line and began to pull steadily, and it may give some idea of its weight that the bow of the inflatable was almost underwater, and the propeller in midair, before the pipe broke the surface.

Once up, we manoeuvred the pipe amidships and dragged the heavily kinked boat sideways beneath it in the direction of the leak. I worried that the barnacles would tear the rubber, and then where would we be, but Grahame was unconcerned and before long we spotted the residual bubbles and heard the faint gurgling, which told us we were in the right place.

I hope James McFerran will forgive me for saying that the obviously aged repair that confronted us had his very distinctive stamp on it. Always resourceful, he had at some time in the past found the same leak, and had effected a repair using two or three rolls of insulating tape, a six-inch piece of reinforced inch-and-a-half plastic hose slit lengthways and slipped snugly around the pipe, and four jubilee clips, two of which in the intervening years had reduced to rust-coloured, deeply waisted impressions of themselves around the circumference of the hose. That this repair, carried out without the assistance of a plumber or even a plumber's merchant, had ensured a supply of water to the island for so long was a tribute to him.

James McFerran is a remarkable man. Now in his mid-eighties, he still actively farms the island, crossing the sound in a little clinker-built dinghy several times a week, in all weathers. I asked him once if he hadn't thought about giving it up and he said simply, 'One day the decision will be taken out of my hands.' May that day be a long way off.

I scraped away the barnacles for a foot on either side of James's repair, and lashed the pipe in two places to the dinghy's wooden seat. Then we held our breath and used a hacksaw to cut out the repaired section entirely. The pipe, thankfully, didn't disappear over the side and I made good with an alcathene connector with special three-quarter-inch adapters.

When we eased the pipe over the bow and let go, it didn't so much sink quietly out of sight as twang like a bowstring, shooting under tension to the bottom and leaving little bits of shell and barnacle flesh behind on the surface of the water.

Unfortunately, the grappling hook went with it, its line somehow entangled with the pipe. Grahame told me not to worry, that he'd dive for it some day; but I bought him a new one anyway, a more elaborate, collapsible contrivance attached by a shackle to six feet of galvanised chain, and presented it to him one afternoon at the pontoons. He was loading provisions from a handcart onto *Sarah May III* and I asked him where he was headed.

'Clockwise round the island.'

'Very good,' I said. 'Have a nice day.'

'*Ireland*,' he said. 'Clockwise round Ireland.'

break fast.

Twenty-eight

Every morning without fail, when I step out through the bedroom window and before my eyes react to the glare of the first struck match of the day, I cross the veranda to the rail and check that the rowing boat, the With and our swimming raft are where they should be: secured, respectively, to the jetty, the mooring and a battered old buoy that somehow continues to stay afloat, swinging precariously on the surface above a seized and rusty fisherman's anchor on permanent loan from John Scott.

Every imaginable variation on what I do *not* want to see has at some point come to pass. Many times the rowing boat has vanished and I have hustled down the jetty in bare feet and pyjama bottoms to find it swamped or even upside down, its contents – oars, duckboards, baling bucket – nowhere to be seen. Typically this is after a change of wind direction in the night, and the failure of the stern anchor to hold in the stones or the mud. The boat swings off the anchor and comes to rest under the jetty; the tide creeps up and traps it there, and eventually something has to give. It tends to be the boat: the free end rises with the tide and hangs in the air, the trapped end creaks and rocks and points reluctantly downwards, water begins to flow in over the gunwales, so – shipwreck. I haul it into the shallows, turn it over or laboriously bale it out, and at first light I go in search of the oars. More often than not I've been lucky, starting with the likeliest beat on the basis of my best guestimate of time of disaster, direction and strength of wind, state of tide. If I can spot one item within the confines of the sound, the others will not be far away; if not, I wish the whole caboodle *bon voyage* and some lucky beachcomber *bonne chance*.

Potentially much more serious, the With herself has wandered off more than once. It has never been the fault of the mooring, which has held faithfully, and I have had to look to my knots. The pretence that something outwith my control – a shackle, a tired rope – is to blame has tended to be unavailable, as the boat, being easier to spot than an oar or a bucket, has been recovered by someone else and the evidence has been plain to see. On one occasion my uncle came down to breakfast to see the With bobbing past his kitchen window in a gale of wind, no one aboard. He kindly – and with no small effort – retrieved her, and embarrassingly enough the bowline, with which I thought I had tied her to the mooring, was still intact and trailing off her bow. In the early hours of the morning I must have grabbed the mooring chain, which is looped near the surface to accept the With's bow rope, and passed the end of the rope through ... what? I never did work it out.

Maybe it's the mooring fairy. Shortly afterwards, it happened again but this time the boat had left the sound altogether. I spent a fruitless hour rowing up and down and finally climbed to the top of Eagle Hill with binoculars. The With was nowhere to be seen but I spotted Norrie Duggan's green fishing boat a mile and a half to the northeast, and thought it worth enquiring. I went to fetch the 5 hp outboard we keep in the shed, and fixed it to the stern of the rowing boat. Much too heavy for the boat, which is only seven feet long, the outboard would take us down by the stern without my counterbalancing weight, so I contrived an extra long tiller arm from an old brush shaft and some insulating tape, settled myself on the buoyancy tank in the bow and headed out into the lough, my erratic line the result of a wide discrepancy between action and reaction: to alter course by two or three degrees I had to move the end of the broom by as many feet.

No doubt intrigued by the white blob weaving its way towards them, the fishing boat had stopped in the water by the time I arrived. I came alongside, and to avoid moving aft and swamping the rowing boat, I stabbed at the gear lever with one of the oars, looking for neutral. I reached up and draped an arm nonchalantly over the fishing boat's gunwale, but as the rowing boat continued to move forwards my arm was forced, pending success with the gear lever, to move with it, bouncing and sliding inelegantly along; and I quickly abandoned my attempt at hard-bitten Bogey-esque ease – in command of the situation, at one with the sea and my little *African Queen* – in order to concentrate on coming to a stop.

I hadn't met Norrie before.

'You would be Norrie,' I said, without looking up. 'I'd shake your hand but I'm trying' (*stab*) 'to find neutral. Would you mind just –'

I was going to ask him to lean over and push the gear lever back a notch, but at that moment the oar hit home and sent the lever all the way through neutral and into reverse. Back we went, away from Norrie's outstretched arm, scudding along the side of his boat and taking some water over the stern. There was nothing for it but to take a step, with its attendant risks, over the middle thwart so that I could operate the controls from closer to. Having no dignity left to hold on to anyway, I felt that sending the boat to the bottom and thus becoming Norrie's most interesting and talked-about catch of the season wasn't really such a bad prospect, and I didn't bother even to look over my shoulder to check out the freeboard. Instead, I motored forward, my bottom somewhere below the water line and my head on a level with the bow, and introduced myself afresh as I came up to the smiling figure of Norrie for the second time.

While he, cheerfully and without comment, took a hold of the rowing boat, I moved back to the relative safety of the middle thwart.

'Mike Faulkner,' I said. 'We're living on Islandmore. You haven't seen a dinghy on your travels, 14 foot? We seem to have lost her off the mooring!'

'I have,' he said. 'Just off Ringdufferin. I put the anchor down and I was going to pick it up on my way back.'

Ringdufferin. Not far. I was surprised I hadn't seen the boat from Eagle Hill; even more surprised that she had drifted south at all, as there had been a light but steady breeze from the southwest since the previous evening. She must have left the mooring between an hour and two hours after high tide, when the ebb was at its strongest – around four knots – strong enough to carry her across the wind. That would mean around midnight. How lucky, I thought, that she hadn't gone any further – Ringdufferin was little more than half a mile away – and that Norrie Duggan had seen her.

I thanked him for his trouble and we talked about the fishing. Half a dozen fish boxes were stacked on the deck behind the wheelhouse, and in the gaps between them I could see the lazy movements of their rather unsavoury – to western tastes anyway – occupants. Whelks, or sea snails (like garden snails but the size of a small fist, with deeply ribbed tan and grey shells) have a ready market in the Far East and these particular ones were likely to end up, apparently, in Japan.

On the way to Ringdufferin to rescue the With (none the worse for her adventure and waiting, half-hidden but floating, amongst the rocks of Ringdufferin Point) it struck me that Ringhaddy's little fishing fleet of three boats might constitute a new resource for us, and I mentioned this to Lynn. She passed on the whelks but we conceived a plan for John and Emma's next visit, organised for the following week. Emma had already suggested a seafood-fest on the island, since her birthday, 7 July, would coincide with their visit, and while the idea had originally been to comb the foreshore as usual for mussels, cockles and oysters, I was beginning to think in terms of a much more elaborate menu to include crab, prawn, and Lynn's personal lifetime favourite of fresh lobster.

As it happened, another boat, another fisherman, came round Eagle Point into the sound a week later, just as we were leaving the jetty to go ashore. I heard *Harvest Home*, as I do every morning, long before she actually appeared, as the engine has a most distinctive, throaty sound. I could say, roar, or blast, or even racket: she has invited all kinds of colourful descriptions from our sleeping guests on her daily exits from the sound at 6 or 7 a.m. Personally, though, I think of her engine note in terms of music – something closer to Guns N' Roses than Gilbert and Sullivan, but there's nothing wrong with that.

As we motored out to meet her, *Harvest Home* slowed down and we made a tight turn to come alongside. I knew Kevin Doherty from the day Grahame Stronge and I had fixed the water pipe running under the sound. He had been on the foreshore, making up a fibreglass patch for his rowing boat, and in the course of conversation had let slip that before turning to fishing for a living he had been a plumber. 'Just the man,' I said; but I had to concede that fibreglassing is a timing-critical business, and indeed that we too were on only a patching mission that afternoon: *plumbing* would be too grand a word and the assistance of an actual plumber, a luxury. Besides, I knew how Kevin felt: twenty-five years after leaving the legal profession, people with any number of family, or employment, or contractual issues will still turn to me and say, '*You're* a lawyer, Mike …'

Kevin cut his engine, making communication a practical possibility, and we allowed the two boats to drift together into the anchorage. I told him what we had in mind: that in two days' time we intended to bring together as many of the lough's resources as possible on one table; that we could manage the three shellfish staples from the foreshore in front of the house, plus, with any luck, a few mackerel; and that for anything more exotic we were hoping to call on his expertise with the creels.

I also asked about the single creel that had mysteriously appeared opposite Lynn's studio, just off our rock, at the beginning of June. At first we had thought nothing of it, but a fortnight went by and we were pretty sure that no one, in that time, had come to lift it. Curiosity eventually got the better of me and I lifted it myself, to find a selection of green crabs in various states of health or dead, and an undersize lobster, still very much alive, which had been there long enough to handcuff itself to the floor of its cage by slipping a claw between two bars, and simply growing ... It was already a full cuff size beyond ever being able to withdraw its claw, which certainly seemed to confirm that the creel had been forgotten, or abandoned, or had fallen off the back of a passing fishing boat.

After slipping the creel door and tipping out the rest of the contents, I tried every possible angle and approach to free the unfortunate creature without losing a finger, and eventually resorted to the With's mud anchor, working its pointed tip between the bars until the trapped claw could pass through. When it did, it was all action for a few moments as I wrestled with the creel, the anchor and, above all, the lobster, who seemed to have a thoroughly ungracious attitude towards being liberated. As the banging and clattering subsided we came face to face on the bottom of the boat, and we each assumed the same defensive position, arms outstretched, claws wide; we circled one another, eye to stalk, and every time I tried to get hold of him from above he grabbed and snapped in the air, rearing and arching on his hind legs, daring me to have a go. *You and whose army*, he seemed to say, but it was all bravado: he hadn't counted on my vastly superior intelligence and my human talent for deviousness. I sprang over him onto the stern seat, and before he could figure out where I'd gone, I had him from behind, dangling him momentarily over the water as he continued to swipe and jab helplessly at thin air.

I turned him around so that I could salute him as a worthy adversary, but he had no appetite for surrender and as I dropped him into the water he was still boiling with rage and indignation and I half-expected him to climb back into the boat.

Well, although Kevin had dropped a creel or two in the area, this one apparently wasn't his. Finders keepers: I decided that when Sam and his parents arrived, we would try our own luck with the salvaged creel. Meantime, as far as local ingredients were concerned, Kevin said he couldn't promise lobster, which were scarce, but that he would see what he could do about eating crabs and prawns.

We agreed to meet him two days later, safe in the knowledge that if all else failed, we could fall back on the dubious delicacy of fresh Strangford Lough sea snails.

the diver

Twenty-nine

Rumour had it that the lough had been alive with mackerel since the end of June – certainly that's what I told John when he arrived. Emma was pleased because she could put a provisional tick against at least one course – hopefully just the starter – of her birthday banquet; but John was palpably excited, and gazed with great meaning over the sound towards the cabin. He narrowed his eyes and swept his hand across the horizon, fingers spread, like Moses at the Red Sea.

'Do we take the boat,' he asked, 'or do we walk across their silvery backs?'

This wasn't sarcasm; this was pure innocent conviction, a born fisherman's belief that *today is the day*. If I should let him down, not to worry: tomorrow would be too.

But this time I had a secret weapon, which I hoped would ensure I did *not* let him down. My cousin-in-law Nial once spent four years fishing the lough commercially. He knew all the dodges, and had fixed me up with a killer fishing rig of his own making; a clever device made from a block of half-inch hardwood eight inches by three, some aluminium channel and a nylon trace complete with four evenly spaced mackerel feathers and a single steel spinner. It was known as an otter board, and when dropped over the stern and trolled at the end of a hand line, it would, he told me, 'swim' below the surface. The fishing depth would be a function of the amount of line paid out, the speed of the boat and, crucially, the point at which the hand line was fixed to the wooden block (there being two fixing points, at one inch and two inches back from the leading edge, for shallow and deep fishing, respectively).

I had never used such sophisticated tackle. If the boat should slow down or make a sharp turn, the otter board would simply float to the surface, removing any worries about catching the bottom; and if the line was taken by a fish, the extra drag would cause it to turn over and 'swim' obligingly back to the surface. Apparently, you could throw the thing over the side, tie off the end of the line and relax. If a little plume of spray appeared fifty yards behind the boat, it was probably dinner.

Thus equipped, the following morning we pushed off from the jetty with high expectations, our mission to catch some bait for the creel and hopefully one or two for the pot: a dress rehearsal for the real thing in two days' time. The sun was strong and the sound so flat calm that every boat, every mooring buoy, had its counterpart below it, and cattle on the sloping fields of the mainland grazed upside down in the water.

We had been told by 'Butch' Mawhinny, another of Ringhaddy's fishermen, that although most people troll for mackerel in the main body of the lough, the narrow entrance to Ringhaddy Sound is in fact one of the most productive runs in the area, especially on a flood tide; so we dropped our line – or rather young Sam dropped *my* line – while still within sight of the cabin.

John and I were still fiddling with the spinning rods, comparing weights and lures and debating whether trolling or jigging was best, when Sam turned to his father with a mildly shocked expression.

'I think I've caught one, Dad.' He stood up and stared at the water and began nodding his head vigorously. 'I have. I've caught one.'

Now to be fair, we had all heard that before, and not just from the youngsters. Our woeful record on their first visit, and mine ever since, had been full of phantom catches. John tore himself away from the much more important business of preparing to catch actual fish, long enough to say something like, 'I think we might find that's a bit of weed, Sam. Pull it in and let's have a look.'

Sam was standing on the seat now. As he was clearly wasting his time with his father, he tried the rest of us in turn, his voice rising, pleading.

'Mum! Lynn! I've caught a fish! Mike! DAD!'

He was screaming now, and I don't know about the others, but I was beginning to take him seriously. Remembering what Nial had said about the otter board coming to the surface, I looked off the stern. I knew right away that our long dry run was over, and that Sam had led his little band of hunters into the wild – and hit pay dirt. The otter board was weaving from side to side, throwing up water just as Nial had described.

'Haul him in, Sam!' I said, and cut the outboard.

Suddenly the back of the boat was crowded. John dropped his fishing rod and went to assist Sam, who was pulling in line for all he was worth, his hands a blur; Emma and little Tom moved back a bench and shouted encouragement. Lynn, predictably, looked the other way, feeling the predicament – and the pain – of the luckless addition to the ship's company who was soon to join us against his will.

When the otter board came alongside the boat, John held the line while Sam reached down to grab the nylon trace. The mackerel had taken the spinner on the end and for a few moments he cruised beside us, almost invisible from above in his blue-green camouflage, the four brightly coloured feathers cruising in line ahead of him; but when he came close to the surface, he darted and dived and fought the line with everything he had, flashing his silver belly, disappearing beneath our feet and then swinging out on a tightly conscribed arc away from the boat. When Sam got hold of the line and yanked it high over his head, the fish twisted and thrashed gamely in midair and thudded onto the seat beside him, swimming hard.

Aware of Lynn's distaste for the next bit, I despatched it as fast as I could with a little brass priest from the stern locker, and for the rest of the morning we gloried in – indeed added to – our triumph. Final tally: John (ably assisted by Tom) 1, Mike 1, Sam 3.

Lunch was on the warm pebbles of Long Sheelah under a beating sun, the water silently, imperceptibly creeping up around us. With the addition of a solitary palm and a shaggy, half-naked old mariner who can't remember how long he's been there, Long Sheelah would be quite the comic-strip desert island – lonely, featureless and far from anywhere; that's to say, sublime.

Our photograph album is full of pictures of the place: Lynn's sister, Fiona, in a summer skirt and bomber jacket, 'fishing', silhouetted against the evening sky, her back arched against an unseen giant of a fish (of the phantom variety), her rod bent almost double; our friend Christine gathering heart-shaped pebbles, or speed-sketching while she chats away, capturing the moment with more honesty than a camera, and almost as fast; her husband, Sean – friend, philosopher, long-term colleague in the furniture business, graduate of my own wheak-it-in school of joinery, and yet another artist – taking offbeat but telling photographs; Lynn with Jock and Rab, the first and second, or second and third loves of her life – I really wouldn't put money on which; Lynn with her mum; Lynn with Andrew and Leslie (who introduced us – already aficionados of Santa Fe, the style – to Santa Fe, the place); Lynn with Allan MacDonald's sister Shona, an artist *and* a singer; Lynn with Jock and Rab, Lynn with Jock and Rab, Lynn with Jock and Rab …

After working our way through the contents of the picnic basket (Sirram, 'made in England since 1895', a wedding present to my parents in 1951), we walked the ever-diminishing length of Long Sheelah between its ever-advancing sides, keeping an eye out behind us in case the island should part company with the boat, before heading home over the same pristine surface on which we had arrived.

Back at Islandmore, before going ashore we baited the creel with one of the mackerel and dropped it, as near as we could tell with the tide so high, at the edge of our rock. Every hour or so until bedtime, Sam asked if perhaps we should check it, but as sensible adults, John and I were prepared to wait; until breakfast time the following day, anyway – Emma's birthday – when there was a scramble to get in the boat and find out what bounty the lough had bestowed.

The day promised to be another scorcher. All of us menfolk were there for the inaugural creel-raising, which revealed a dozen of the same small greenish-blue crabs – known, Kevin told us, as 'velvets' – which we discarded, a much larger brown one (I said, 'That's an eater, isn't it?' and John said, 'Yes. How did you know its name was Anita?') and, of all things, a dogfish. This last I treated as something of a novelty, holding it up by the tail so the boys could get a good look at its shark-like jaws, before throwing it back in the water. John was appalled, and for days we argued about whether dogfish was a rare delicacy or a filthy scavenger. I looked it up in a pocket guide to the sea and invoked the Latin name of at least one kind of dogfish, *Squalus acanthius*, in support of my argument, but in the end, as usual, John had the final word. Six months later he sent me a book for Christmas, *The World Encyclopaedia of Fish and Shellfish* by Kate Whiteman, with this inscription on the flyleaf:

Dear Mike:
For future reference please see pages 70–71.
Happy Christmas, John

I turned to page 70:

Dogfish has good firm flesh and can be cooked in the same ways as monkfish and skate. It is excellent in casseroles and is the perfect fish for fish and chips. This fish can also be grilled or barbecued with a good coating of olive oil, or cooked and flaked and used in salads. Dogfish is delicious smoked.

Not a particularly versatile or good-eating fish, then.

Well, dogfish may have been off the menu for Emma's birthday feast through crass prejudice and ignorance on my part, but so far we had four mackerel, as many cockles, mussels and oysters as we could gather on the foreshore, and Anita. A promising start, and we were eager to see what Kevin might turn up with later.

To put it mildly, he didn't disappoint. When we saw, or rather heard him coming round the point, we took the With out to meet him, and it was obvious from the smile on his face that he had something special for us. He heaved a box onto the shooting tray on the side of his boat so that we could see inside and said: 'That suit you?'

We had thought that Anita was a good size but Kevin had caught a crab that was ... bigger, much bigger. If I hadn't read that in the waters off Japan there are spider crabs with a claw-span of three metres, I would have said it was prodigious. Later we measured the shell at a tad under ten inches. Keeping it company were two good-size lobsters and a couple of dozen prawns. Kevin pointed at the boxes behind him and said, 'Whelks?' and despite doubtful looks from the others, I said, 'Why not?' – and a few were duly added to the haul.

I noticed that he also had a box or two of velvets, the little crabs we had discarded earlier along with the dogfish.

'The Spanish eat them with white wine,' he said. 'Like a few?'

The velvets, funny enough, were the only thing we passed on, reckoning that with all the prising and picking we had already let ourselves in for, they were hardly worth the effort given their diminutive size. It's a treat, in fact, that still awaits us.

As Kevin wouldn't accept payment, we handed over a rather paltry two bottles of wine and a box of chocolates, thanked him profusely and assured him we would let him know how we got on.

Back on the veranda, we were all given jobs by Lynn. The boys were handed buckets and sent for cockles and mussels; John donned my chest waders and went after oysters; Lynn and Emma took on the table and planned cooking operations; and I was put in charge of the barbecue and, rather unfairly, the whelks: 'You took them, you do something with them,' Lynn said with a bright smile, and handed me a bulging carrier bag.

It all came together beautifully. By the time we were ready to eat, the sun was low in the sky but the air was still warm, scented with hawthorn smoke from the barbecue. As always at that time of the evening, a pair of ravens talked quietly and with great variety between themselves in the topmost branches of the nearest pine. Lynn had covered the table with a white linen cloth borrowed from my mother and reserved for special occasions. The centrepiece was a chunk of driftwood inset with candles. On two enormous platters were arranged the *fruits de mer*, lobsters and crabs on one, everything else on the other; and between them, a wooden bowl piled high with salad leaves glistening in the candlelight. The barbecue was reserved, with high hopes and some lateral thinking on John's part, for the oysters: rather than open them by hand our plan was to pop them on the barbecue and let them open themselves, a plan that, in fact, worked perfectly.

When the platters were empty, we took our coffee and sat on the grass around the circle of stones which made up the barbecue, and Lynn came down the wooden steps in the half-light, her face set aglow by the single candle on her birthday speciality – fallen chocolate cake, rich and indulgent – which she carried ceremoniously in front of her. We sang happy birthday to Emma, and there's every reason to think that it was.

Next morning when we cleared up, it was hard to believe that we had eaten our way through so much, but the evidence was there in the shape of two big bowls of discarded shells that had overspilled onto the table.

Alas, you can't have everything. Off to the side – sampled, rejected, abandoned – was a plateful of shelled, lightly grilled and seasoned-with-a-dash-of-Tabasco by Yours Truly ... Strangford Lough whelks.

Thirty

Both being dedicated foodies – well, I would tend towards consumption rather than production, while Lynn is at home with either – we love to dine out and have always enjoyed the adventure of interesting eateries with imaginative menus.

Our tastes are fairly eclectic but there is one constant to which, in frequent need of a chile hit, we often seem to return. Having acquired a taste for New Mexican cuisine and finding that it was unavailable outside our own kitchen (and, to be fair, the kitchen of our friend Leslie, who served the best and whose family connection with the Land of Enchantment has ensured an uninterrupted supply of sun-dried chiles, sopapilla mix and Indian posole – corn – even to Islandmore), we compromised and scoured Edinburgh for a cantina that served a good quality version of New Mexican's less sophisticated progenitor, Mexican. We found only one, the modest Blue Parrot on St Stephen Street, which consistently managed all the essentials: atmosphere, fresh ingredients, the right amount of heat, margaritas made with freshly squeezed limes and good tequila, and of course friendly and unobtrusive service. We introduced them to chipotle (smoked jalapeño) chile and they have had an alternative salsa on the menu ever since, which we invariably order.

Lynn's chipotle sauce, incidentally, is made as follows: soak 10 dried smoked chiles in hot water to soften (approximately 30 minutes); finely chop 1 medium onion and 5 garlic cloves, and soften in a pan with oil; add 4 tablespoons of vinegar and 5 of tomato puree, the juice of a lime, a pinch of salt and 3 cups of water. Simmer together with the softened chiles for an hour, and purée. *Buen provecho!* It's hot, so a little goes a long way – a tablespoon added to a bowl of Greek yoghurt makes a good dip and works well with salmon or mussels.

Since coming to the island, on the lookout for places to treat our guests – or for them to treat us – we have worked our way around the perimeter of the lough trying anything droppable-into by boat. For wholesome food, live music, or both, we have enjoyed Fiddler's Green in Portaferry (the lunchtime rendition of 'The Secondhand Trousers I Bought in Belcoo', so enjoyed by John Hawkins and myself, and to a lesser extent by young Tom, was but a taster for the full-on Irish nights they run from Friday to Sunday from 9 p.m.); and the Dufferin Arms in Killyleagh. On one memorable Saturday evening in the Dufferin we took a table for seven and ate very well while regulars Charlie Magoran (guitar), David Lowray (banjo), William Garrett (Irish pipes) and Tracy McGookin (mandolin), joined by some prodigiously talented drop-in musicians, gave us an excellent selection of Irish traditional, bluegrass and country, including Johnny Cash's 'Blue Eyes', and at the insistence of Magoran himself, the wonderfully named Jimmy Delaney ('like the donkey') sang – in line with the 'eyes' theme around which I thought, for a while, the evening had been built – 'Beautiful Brown Eyes' a capella from the floor, to an appreciatively silenced audience. Live music at the Dufferin is on Saturdays, from late afternoon to late.

As for restaurants and cafés, it's a mixed and perhaps inconsistent bag, but it's always fun no matter how bad – in one case, where the salade niçoise had all the essentially niçoise ingredients of anchovies, olives and tuna with the exception of the anchovies, olives or the tuna, it was fun *because* it was so bad – and as I mentioned before, we have had some excellent meals at Portaferry Hotel and The Narrows.

So, after painstaking first-hand and necessarily subjective research, here is a list of places that tick all the following boxes: fresh local ingredients; nice location, good atmosphere, comfortable seating; consistently excellent food with adventurous combinations; regularly changing, flexible menu; good value for money; real cappuccinos made with good coffee; invested, hands-on, friendly owners; interested, helpful, on-the-ball staff; outside seating area.

1 Picnic Delicatessen, 47 High Street, Killyleagh.

John and Kath Dougherty met while he was running a smokehouse on Rothiemurchus Estate near Aviemore, Scotland, and she was travelling in Europe. Back home in Melbourne, Kath had run a number of restaurants, so they had good food in common but it's fair to say they took their time to get together. John returned to his native Northern Ireland and Kath returned to her native Australia. Eight years later, after an inordinate amount of corresponding and travelling, they married and settled in Northern Ireland, and in due course combined their passions for food in this delightful café delicatessen in the shadow of Killyleagh Castle.

The menu changes daily but here is a flavour:

Sweet potato and pear soup with ginger mascarpone
Spicy peanut soup

Focaccia with roast chicken, chiles, mango chutney,
cheese and roasted red peppers
Grilled halloumi, parma ham and salad with kiwi,
lime and tangerine dressing
Greek stefado – beef with feta cheese, fresh basil, pine nuts
and soft flour tortilla
Italian polenta pie with sweet potato (dairy- and wheat-free)
Herrings and warm chorizo salad with oatcakes

Portuguese custard tart
Fallen chocolate cake
Chocolate, apricot and brandy brownies

Irish, French and Italian cheeses

Produce sold in the deli section, like the lunch menu, changes all the time but is fresh, interesting, sometimes quirky. Verdict: excellent; breath of fresh air; wish they opened in the evening.

2 That's it really.

turquoise boat, yellow man

Thirty-one

Not being much of a guy's guy – always, in fact, having been more at home in the company of women and the elderly – I was happy to find myself, on a balmy afternoon in August, outnumbered six to one and heading off to explore the string of little islands that lies beyond Dunsy.

Puddleduck was there, of course; also our friend Sara, a novelist from Edinburgh who has the enviable talent of being able to sit down and just *write*. For an hour one morning she sat with her notebook on the grass in front of the cabin, propped against the wooden fence with her back to the sea, and when I asked later how she'd got on, she said, 'Fine, I was only aiming for five or six hundred words anyway.'

Sara's eleven-year-old daughter, Molly, and her friend, Megan, sat together in the bow, sharing private jokes, and we stopped by to pick up my recently be-teened first cousin (once removed) Alice from the mainland foreshore in front of her parents' house at the north end of Ringhaddy Sound. Orchard House occupies, I should think, one of the finest positions on the lough, high above the sound on the Castle Island peninsula, with unimpeded views covering almost half the compass from south to just east of north. Sheltered from the prevailing wind and only ever exposed to the less frequent northeasterlies and easterlies, it is the perfect base for a highly specialised business which, in springtime, carpets the south-facing slopes behind the house in yellow – more accurately, yellow, orange, pink, peach, white, apricot, terracotta and every subtlety of hue in between. Trading as Ringhaddy Daffodils, Alice's parents, Nial and Hilary Watson, supply customers as far apart as Japan and Venezuela, and it tickles me to think that their bulbs, which sell for anything from five pounds to eighty pounds apiece and have wonderful names like Silent Valley, Quiet Waters, Knowing Look, and my special favourites from across the pond, Oregon Pioneer and Kokopeli, start their journey in this quiet corner of Ireland and might even have been touched by Lynn's fair hand during one of her brief stints with Nial and his team of helpers.

We toured the archipelago of islands – Green Island, Great Minnis, Little Minnis, Drummond and the beautifully named Inishanier and Inisharoan – looking for a picnic site. We landed briefly at the southwest corner of Green Island to inspect the stone ruins of its kelp house, where for more than a century, from the early 1700s to the mid-1800s, kelp was stored after being harvested from the shores of nearby islands on a carefully managed three-year rotational cycle, dried on the grass and reduced to sodium-rich ash in open kilns just above the foreshore, before being despatched for use in glass and soap manufacture and, most importantly, as a bleaching agent for the growing Irish linen industry.

We settled on the northeast side of Green Island, where a steep, terraced slope, the result of wave erosion during a period of higher sea levels towards the end of the last Ice Age, offered sun as well as spectacle and a good bed of coarse grass to sit on. The others went ahead of me while I tied three ropes together so that the With could lie off. I jammed her anchor between two boulders and put my foot to her bow, shoving her off as hard as I could; then followed the others up the hill.

As is my habit, I glanced over my shoulder to see that all was well with the boat. It wasn't. The With was slipping further offshore than could possibly be explained, even by the three-rope daisy chain I had painstakingly tied, and I realised with a sick feeling that she wasn't going to stop. With no time to work out which of six interlocking bowlines I had neglected to make good, I stripped to my underpants and began vaulting and tripping and scrambling my ungainly way across the twenty yards or so of weed-covered boulders that separated me from the water.

Just before diving in I felt a stabbing pain in the sole of my right foot, and then it was all blind exertion, the taste of saltwater and an overdue realisation that I was no longer sixteen, as I pursued the boat across the sound that separates Green Island from Great Minnis – perhaps a quarter of a mile of open water – and was forced, gradually, to accept that the gap between us was widening. The breeze had caught the boat and despite a final burst of speed – 'speed' being such a relative term – I had to let her go.

Meanwhile, back on Green Island Puddleduck had been taking photographs, and three of them tell the story from the girls' perspective. The first is all picnic rugs, laughter and fun.

In the second, taken ten minutes into my swim, all faces have turned to the sea and the smiles have gone; Lynn, in particular, has a dark and stony expression I have never seen before.

And the third photograph shows the Green Island shoreline and the sound, with the Minnises in the background: the With, empty and looking a little lost, is off to the northwest, halfway between the two islands, and I am a pink and grey spot somewhat to southeast of her. It looks to be the point immediately after I have decided to abandon the chase, because my head is

pointing in the direction of Great Minnis and slightly away from the boat.

In point of fact I was beginning to struggle. I had in mind that if the With continued her languid journey on the same general course, she would probably fetch up on the southwest corner of Great Minnis; and that if I took the shortest route to shore, I could make my way along to her on dry land. For the moment, though, I was winded and running out of strength and I really began to wonder if I had it in me

to make the shore. There was a little too much wave to float on my back, so I decided to tread water for a while and try to get my breath back, a strategy that worked well enough but apparently frightened the life out of Lynn, to whom it appeared that I had simply stopped, and was sinking.

Odd and irrational thoughts come into your mind at times like this. My right foot hurt with every downward stroke and when dark swirls began to vein the water around me, I thought *blood*; and in turn, *sharks*. As a fisherman named Luke Turkington from the far side of the lough will confirm, that is not as silly as it sounds, because he was curious enough to send photographs of the half-eaten remains of a young porpoise for laboratory analysis to be told, in due course, that it had probably been attacked by porbeagle sharks. Porbeagles, in the same family as great whites, have been seen in warmer British waters (off Cornwall, for example) for years, but rarely this far north, and one theory is that certain shark species have begun to extend their territorial range in response to global temperature shifts; that we are, in fact, likely to see more of them.

When you're bleeding from the foot and treading water, these are dark thoughts, so while I could have said that somewhere deep inside I found the strength to go on, that would be misleading: I know very well where I found the strength and, if anything, I covered the second half of my journey in shorter order than the first. Even when I got into the shallows on Great Minnis, I kept an eye on the water behind me, images courtesy of David Attenborough crowding my mind of unsuspecting sea lions, killer whales and that innocuous-looking beach on the other side of the world.

The With and I seemed to have struck the island at more or less the same time and a few hundred yards apart. I minced my way along the foreshore towards her, stepping gingerly between the sharp stones, favouring my gashed foot and holding up my sodden underpants with one hand: hardly the picture of the heroic saviour I would like to have projected for the girls, who were standing up and waving from the hill across the sound. Nevertheless, having recaptured the boat and motored back to Green Island, I was afforded a hero's welcome by Molly and Megan, who wrapped me up in towels and made a proper fuss over me. Alice, quietly solicitous as always, pressed a mug of tea into my hand and Puddleduck contrived an ingenious dressing for my bleeding foot using the barcode sticker from a punnet of Sainsbury's strawberries; and through the explanations and the apologies and the animated — perhaps exaggerated — reprise of events that followed, I kept looking at Lynn and thinking, Never again … And she kept looking at me, pointing a figurative finger and saying back, without a word: *Never again!*

If picnics were always this eventful, we would have used up nine lives in as many weeks over our first summer, or at least I would. But our photograph album, and my journal, are so full of easy hours stretched out on the wind-flattened grass of remote rocks and islands, surrounded by sea pinks, cow parsley and wild irises, the smell of salt and the sounds of the sea, that in retrospect I wonder how we got anything done. It was a time to consolidate and to enjoy old friendships, particularly with those we left behind, and we found that because we tended to set aside a few days to justify their journeys from Scotland, the time we spent together had more substance, unhurried and largely untrammelled, as it was, by the social niceties of arrival times, polite greetings and small talk.

And of course most of our friends, never having lived on a bona fide island, have been on adventures of their own, giving us the double pleasure of providing and sharing. It can be a culture shock for them, there's no doubt about it. There is something either magical or unsettling, depending on your point of view, in the knowledge that the strip of water in front of you is more than just a strip of water, as in a river or a freshwater loch. For some it represents an unnatural, perhaps even scary, suspension of normal life, but for us it is a barrier on the other side of which we have been able to take leave of the rest of the world without appearing unfriendly. The drawbridge, on an island, is always raised and there's no need to feel guilty about it: it is raised by the hand of creation. No one is going to drop by unannounced or even invite themselves casually in advance; both of which, I appreciate, may be the mainstays of another couple's social life.

Above all, for Lynn and me the island has been a place of healing. If our little life reversal tested our relationship, it never threatened it, and we have been able to make the most of island life together. Through the island-tinted lens of a double seebackroscope, which had gathered dust for far too long, we have learned to look forward again. Lynn's work is more confident and inspired than ever, and I have rediscovered a nascent urge to 'put it in writing'. A little inarticulate, a lot shy, I have always been more comfortable with the written than the spoken word, and we all share the need to communicate.

And if I have been tempted to link my business difficulties with the sneaking feeling that I was never the sharpest tack in the stationery

drawer, the island has brought home to me that intelligence comes in a number of different but equally workable configurations, of which at least one has much to do with can-do and common sense. I asked an old school friend recently whether the fact that we were in class 4C together meant that we were stupid, and he said: 'No, just different.'

That's fine then.

Thirty-two

We cannot live on Islandmore for ever. My mother's name is on the deeds and in every other sense the cabin belongs to the whole family.

My mother has often said that after losing my father she saw herself primarily as custodian. Without him, the cabin, like music and painting, had little appeal and for many years she was reluctant to return to the place at all, so full was it of painful memories. When she did come to stay with us in July, it was the first time she had slept there in twenty-five years, and she surprised herself by enjoying the experience. It prompted the ultimate endorsement, the one that accompanied every positive decision, every new direction taken by herself or her children since 3 March 1977: 'It would please your father.'

When I think of my mother on the island in the old days, I smell oil paint and turpentine; indeed when I smell oil paint and turpentine (not unusual when you marry into the community of artists), I think of my mother. If Lynn hadn't opted for acrylics while she was at art college, I would probably live in a state of time-bending confusion, so powerful is the trigger of that particular olfactory imprint.

一

199

It was my mother's habit to take her easel over the hills on Islandmore. She would spend whole days in blissful absorption and thanks to her talents we now have a number of fine views of the sound from the days before boat congestion, car parks and concrete walkways. Ringhaddy will always be a lovely spot but in those days it was a well-kept and well-respected secret and we knew ourselves to be among the privileged few.

The four of us used to go and seek my mother out – armed, of course, with a picnic. Da would make great show of preparing tea: he had one of those miraculous water-heating devices that consisted of a double-walled tin sleeve open at both ends, about eighteen inches long and six wide. The walls were filled with water and a single page of rolled up newspaper was stuffed into the sleeve and lit at one end. By the time the paper was reduced to ash the water was boiling. Can it really have been that simple?

On my mother's painting days, if my father wasn't messing about with boats or performing the tea ceremony, he would sit on the veranda with Woodhouse, Delderfield or Somerville and Ross. *Experiences of an Irish R.M.* was his favourite reading and it made him laugh aloud every time he returned to it – which was a great many times, as it so uniquely captured the characters, the humour, the science and the thrill of his life's abiding passion: hunting. He was master and huntsman of a pack of harriers (later foxhounds) for the last seventeen years of his life, and although a kill was a rarity even when game was plentiful (I was brought up with hunting and don't, in fact, remember witnessing a single instance), that was of no concern to my father because it was of no interest to him. His interest was in the ancient and subtle art of working a pack of hounds, of so disposing and encouraging them that they found, and then held, a line of scent; and no more than that. His horse was simply a means of staying with hounds when they were hunting hard; obstacles, in the form of dense County Down thorn hedges with invisible ditches or impossible-looking drops – or both – were no more than hindrances in the pursuit of the same end; and the rest of the field – farmers, lawyers, shopkeepers – were kindred spirits for whom he had all the time in the world before and after a hunt, and none at all during. As with everything he undertook, he was utterly focused when he was hunting hounds; so focused that when he and his long-time friend and predecessor as huntsman, Albert Uprichard, dismounted one day to tackle a particularly stubborn gate, it took my mother to point out some time later that they were riding each other's horses.

The same focus meant he was able to compartmentalise his life, to give all to the job in hand before switching to the next completely and at will, calling whenever necessary on a mysterious mental time-clock that always amazed me. I remember sitting with my parents in the sun room at Seaforde. Da had done some research on Canadian work permits and he was telling me about it when he reached over and turned on the radio without looking at his watch. Five short beeps and one long. 'The World at One: the latest news headlines this Tuesday lunchtime.' After the headlines, he turned off the radio and carried on as before. Perhaps with more far-reaching implications, he frequently scheduled Wednesday Cabinet meetings for the morning during the winter hunting season, and after wrapping up Cabinet business, he would step into the back of the car in his suit and tie and emerge, an hour later, in britches and hunt coat at the meet, where my mother would be waiting for him, riding one horse and leading another.

For the family, he dropped everything; family *was* everything. I doubt whether he ever missed a school sports day, a pony club gymkhana, a birthday party – even if he could only show a face. In the week before Christmas, my mother always took us to see Santa Claus in Anderson & McAuley, the venerable, long-gone department store in the centre of Belfast; and afterwards, more exciting even than Santa's grotto, we would meet my father for tea in the rather gracious second-floor dining room, looking down through a spider's web of intersecting cables at the trolleybuses, and the long electric contacts that bounced and sparked above them.

I only ever remember my father's talent for compartmentalisation failing him once, and for good reason. We happened to be on the island at the beginning of August 1971. The previous seven months had seen the most vicious and sustained violence in the Troubles up to that point and my father, as prime minister with responsibility for Home Affairs, and therefore security, had sought the views of the police, the army and his Cabinet colleagues as to the most effective government response. There being only one important unused weapon left in the armoury of the security forces, these consultations increasingly centred on the single issue of internment without trial for suspected terrorists.

During those few days on the island, we scarcely saw my father and when we did it was obvious to us that he was deeply preoccupied. Too professional ever to confide such matters to the family at large, he nevertheless spent a good deal of time in quiet discussion with my mother. That was inevitable, since over the years they had developed a unique modus operandi that drew on both their talents, and it would have been unthinkable to exclude her. My mother, having trained as a journalist and with natural writing flair, used to work up many of my father's political speeches, which he would in turn reduce to short handwritten headings before delivering them with his trademark clarity and conviction. They were an effective team, and I know that on the morning of 4 August my mother was broadly aware of the course of the coming day before it was formally embarked upon.

For my part, I could only guess, but I knew it was going to be a big one. It is the only time I ever remember feeling sorry for my father. We had an unusually quiet family breakfast and then he kissed my mother goodbye. He was wearing his pinstripe suit and Royal North of Ireland Yacht Club tie. A white handkerchief, folded into a single peak, protruded, as always, from his breast pocket. He walked down the jetty with his briefcase in his hand and his black oilskin coat folded over his arm. Small at the best of times, he looked even smaller then. He had made his decision and would fly to London that morning from RAF Aldergrove to seek formal approval from Downing Street. Having got it, the die was cast, but there was no announcement for a further four days because until just an hour or two before the dawn operation on 9 August, when 342 terrorist suspects were arrested, only a handful of people knew that internment was imminent.

It must have been such a black time for him. He personally reviewed the evidence on every detention order he was asked to sign, and he demurred if he wasn't satisfied in particular cases: of those first 342 arrested he ordered the release of 104. By nature and conviction he found the idea of internment without trial anathema in a modern democracy, but these were dark days for Northern Ireland and my father was a pragmatist, listening to the security advice he was given. In the mid-morning press conference following the arrests, he had this to say to the world's press:

I ask those who will quite sincerely consider the use of internment powers as evil to answer honestly this question: is it more of an evil than to allow the perpetrators of these outrages to remain at liberty?

Bearing in mind that if you extrapolate the figures from Northern Ireland for the first seven months of 1971 (55 dead and more than 600 injured, 320 explosions and 300 shooting incidents) and apply them to the UK population as a whole, you arrive at 2,000 dead, 22,000 injured, 11,000 bombings and 11,600 shootings, he had an argument.

Some years ago my mother asked – silly question – whether I would like to have one of her paintings, a still life of my father's boots, cap and hunt coat, which used to hang above the toilet in her cloakroom.

The painting's position was not accidental: like Lynn, my mother has always been averse to hanging her own work, so it was lucky to be anywhere. It's a beautiful piece, though, and visitors had often commented on the detail and realism she managed to achieve. Someone said, 'You could step into those boots', and I smiled at the presumption – if only – but they were right; it is a tour de force and all the more powerful because each well-worn element of the composition (he was wearing the same boots and cap when he had his accident) was so much a part of my father's life. If there is any comfort in the manner of his going, it is that he went doing what he loved best.

Thirty-three

I was introduced to Canada's favourite poet, Robert Service, when my mother gave me his collected works while I was still at school.

Service grew up in Scotland and emigrated to western Canada in 1895 in time to witness the Klondike Gold Rush of 1897–8. His fertile imagination was fired by what he found there. Dawson City, where the Klondike and Yukon rivers meet, was the gateway to the gold fields of the High North, and Service watched as a human tidal wave rolled in from the south, engulfing the little frontier town and its ramshackle collection of timber buildings and tents. He recorded what he saw – the starry-eyed speculators, the ne'er-do-wells, the hopefuls, the hopeless, the whores – in a series of lyrical poems that always told a story, and always with a smile. The smile was the product of humanity as often as humour: and hopeless romantic that I am, 'The Man from Eldorado' has had me in tears and 'The Ice-Worm Cocktail' in stitches. His descriptions of the characters and their lonely winter treks, of instant fortunes and ignominious failure, were set against the backdrop of an unforgiving country whose beauty held him in thrall, and informed by a deep respect for the courage of those who dared to challenge it – and to hold to their dreams.

On a cold November morning something over twenty years ago, I was sitting alone in the apartment of a friend in Montreal, listening to the radio. Country. My taste in music seems to follow my taste in poetry. Campbell was working, so I had the day to myself. A little restless, I wandered outside and along the sidewalk between banks of earth-coloured snow to the 7-Eleven on the corner; bought some barbecue flavour peanuts and wandered back.

As I opened the door Willie Nelson was singing 'Moonlight in Vermont', and on impulse I lifted the phone and booked myself on a flight to Whitehorse, Yukon Territory, leaving next day. There was a stopover in Calgary, where I picked up a solo tent, a rucksack and a fur-trimmed parka from Mountain Equipment Co-op; and at the airport, two paperback volumes of Service's poems: *Songs of a Sourdough* and *Ballads of a Cheechako*.

I meant to hitch the fifteen hundred miles, in no particular hurry, back to Calgary via the Alaska Highway. I wanted to see something of what Service had seen, and the time of year ensured that in some sense I did: by way of warning that the Yukon winter is meant for loggers and miners only, not a single vehicle passed me in the first few hours of unpaved highway south of Whitehorse; heavy snow followed a short spell of blinding sunshine; and I found myself in a silent, snowy vastness of lakes and hills and trees.

I couldn't have been happier. Come dusk, having refused rides from the two pick-ups that did come along, I left the road and followed a track through the trees. It opened into a clearing, a meadow, on the edge of which were three or four enormous stacks of logs, each the size of a small house. At the far side of the meadow there was a solitary jack pine, and trudging towards it through the snow, I heard running water. The pine, it turned out, was at the top of a steep bank that ran down to the black waters of a fast-flowing river; beyond which, more trees: spruce, larch and, every so often, the hot splash of a single golden tamarack, aflame even in the gathering darkness.

I cleared away a patch of snow under the tree and pitched my tent. By torchlight, with snow piling against the canvas, I wrote a long letter to Lynn, with whom I was, as they say in Ireland, walking out, and another to my mother; and learned by heart the first few verses of 'The Cremation of Sam McGee':

> There are strange things done in the midnight sun
> By the men who moil for gold;
> The Arctic trails have their secret tales
> That would make your blood run cold.
> The Northern Lights have seen queer sights
> But the queerest they ever did see,

Was the night on the marge of Lake Lebarge
I cremated Sam McGee ...

In the morning the world was horizontally divided – clean, hard
blue above, soft white all around – and side-lit by shafts of early sun
cutting through the trees from the east. The little river, black the night
before, had turned silver. I climbed down there and stretched out on
my belly to drink; turned over and lay on my back, staring up. My
own private heaven.

I lingered until hunger called, then dragged myself back to the
highway and, with fortune still smiling, a truck ride to breakfast.

Looking back, I regret that Lynn wasn't there to share my Yukon
adventure with me. I knew even then that it would be her heaven too;
that by the purest good luck I had found a partner who shared the
same dream. Conceptually speaking, that campsite in the middle of
nowhere has our name on it. Ticking the important boxes – *wild,
water, paint, write* – it gives proper weight to place as opposed to
people, by which I mean that having acquired a small circle of good
friends through shared interests, we have no particular ambition to
expand it: good friends and family will always be there.

I see the same forest clearing in the viewing window of my double
seebackroscope, and tramping along the Alaska Highway in the early
winter snow, committing a few of Service's poems to memory, I
found that every line suggested something of a kindred spirit:

Let us probe the silent places, let us seek what luck betide us;
Let us journey to a lonely land I know,
There's a whisper on the night-wind, there's a star agleam to
    guide us,
And the wild is calling, calling ... let us go.

My father, who tended always to think *concrete* rather that *concept*,
would hardly have taken such dewy-eyed sentimentality seriously,
but if life is about balance I can say that he provided an ideological
counterweight without which I would never have got anything
done. He used to say that faced with a difficult decision a person can
do the right thing, the wrong thing or nothing at all; and that it is
sometimes better to do the wrong thing than nothing at all. When

business first began to go awry for us, some time before we finally called it a day, I was advised to contract and consolidate. Instead, I doubled the sales area, built a virtual film set in the street and introduced a sceptical and conservative Edinburgh public to the furniture of the American desert frontier. Perhaps it was the wrong thing to do but it was the most exciting experiment of my business career, and I think my father would be happy to hear me say that I would do the same again. It may have been in his nature, when things went wrong, to say 'Next time ...'; but not, I think, 'In retrospect ...'

Self-evidently my father was a doer and Robert Service a dreamer. Nevertheless, they share wall space, politician and poet, in the Great Hall of my gallery of heroes, between my mother, the font of all wisdom, and Willie Edgar, the inventor and keeper of the double seebackroscope. I like to think that when Willie agreed, in his gentle and protective way, to build me a pair of these legendary instruments, he was really offering me the means to accommodate the philosophies of two very different men.

'Don't just stand there,' he seemed to say. 'Dream a little!'

I do. I always have done but I didn't realise it was acceptable behaviour. And Islandmore is the perfect place to indulge. Not only is there physical separation and the space to sit, and look, and listen, but nature seems always to be in a state of kaleidoscopic shift, encouraging some outlandish flights of fancy. In the most meteorologically freakish experience of our time on the island, Lynn and I stepped into the dinghy from the jetty early one autumn morning – and flew to the mainland above cloud level, catching only occasional glimpses of the water. A foot-high layer of dense mist clung to the surface of Ringhaddy Sound, such that we joined the seagulls as they glided between sawn-off yachts and dinky orange UFOs with steel rings on top, as in a dream; halfway to heaven, our feet below sea level.

It comes as a mild surprise to both of us that we are entering our fourth winter on Islandmore. When we came, we reckoned on a year or two at most; but with each new season the comfortable realisation has grown that should we leave the place for half a lifetime and return in our dotage, never mind that in the meantime we may have lived by a peaty Highland lochan, the blue Mediterranean or the icy rush of a Yukon river, we will always be coming home.

When we do leave the island, we will leave some good friends behind, and to borrow a phrase from Alistair Cooke (who had his human friends in mind) it will hurt to miss them. Our most dependable, if seasonal, neighbours here (excepting Mr Heron), a pair of little grebes – dumpy, buffish, unassuming – have just returned for the winter. They were here when we arrived for our first winter, and they will stay in the sound until early March. The busiest, most energetic of divers, when they are feeding they spend more time below than above the water. Watching them with binoculars from the living-room window requires good guesswork and fast reactions; they will pop up, shake their heads, swallow and dive in the space of a few seconds. They get on with life. Their diving beat exactly corresponds to the length of the cabin and Lynn's studio combined, and if they don't appear in the early morning, working the area of knotted wrack and popweed on either side of the jetty, we begin to worry: roosting waterfowl are the staple of the island's fox population, and if anything happened to them, we would miss them greatly. Like the tides, they are part of the rhythm of the island.

Perhaps, if we stay here long enough, we will be too. In the meantime, like the High North for Services's thin-blooded hero, who begged to be cremated because he couldn't stand the cold ('Sam McGee was from Tennessee, where the cotton blooms and blows'), the island continues, despite its little inconveniences, to hold us like a spell.

Author's Note

My thanks to Isobel Dixon at Blake Friedmann Literary Agency, whose guidance gave the project form and direction; everyone at Blackstaff Press (including Rachel McNicholl, who has since moved on) for their expertise, enthusiasm and forbearance; Hilary Bell, whose sure and sensitive editing was so valuable; Christine Kingsley for her wonderful line drawings; and the Arts Council of Northern Ireland for its generous grant assistance.

A few friends were kind enough to read the manuscript at an early stage; I'm grateful to each of them and particularly to Sara Sheridan, Pam Bevan and Lynn's aunt, Ella Rhude, in Canada.

Thanks also to Alan Franklin of Manx National Heritage Library; Frances Coakley, editor of *A Manx Notebook* (www.manxnotebook.com); The Shark Trust; Irish Whale and Dolphin Group; my uncle Sir Dennis Faulkner; John Houston; Colin Leslie; Philippe Peron; and David Willington.

For stepping generously aside when we moved into the cabin, foregoing some of their own island times, and being so supportive, I want to thank my brother, David, sister-in-law Gail, Lucinda, Jamie and Rory. To my sister, Claire, I would like to say how much I have valued her unshakeable belief. Above all I want to thank my mother, who made the cabin available to us, cast her expert eye over every line in her capacity as unpaid Editor-in-Chief, and infected me with her love of writing.

Very sadly Bob Scott, whose presence I felt so much during the writing of this book, passed away in December 2005, but of no one can it more fittingly be said, that 'the legend lives on'. Also no longer with us – Jock, our Cairn terrier, who died the previous August. He is buried behind the cabin on the high grass bank overlooking the sound, so he will always be there to welcome us back.

Finally, my love and thanks to my wife, Lynn, for whom, in many ways, this book was written.

List of Illustrations

THE SEQUEL TO THE BLUE CABIN

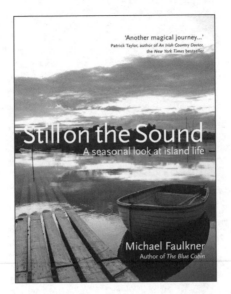

When Mike Faulkner, his wife Lynn and their two dogs first
crossed Ringhaddy Sound to the Blue Cabin on an island in
Strangford Lough, they planned to stay for a year.
Seven years later, the island's magic hasn't lost its hold …

With stormy midnight crossings, dramatic sea rescues and the general
inconveniences of living in a wooden cabin on an Irish sea lough,
life there wouldn't be for everyone, but, for Lynn and Mike,
the compensations are manifold and glorious. *Still on the Sound*
celebrates the seasons, the wildlife and the joy of living on
an otherwise uninhabited island.

Illustrated with more than two hundred of Mike's own colour
photographs, *Still on the Sound* is warm, funny and irresistible
– a love letter to the island.

978-0-85640-849-6
£14.99